CW00540012

797,885 Books

are available to read at

www.ForgottenBooks.com

---◆---

Forgotten Books' App
Available for mobile, tablet & eReader

ISBN 978-1-331-48515-5
PIBN 10196519

This book is a reproduction of an important historical work. Forgotten Books uses
state-of-the-art technology to digitally reconstruct the work, preserving the original format
whilst repairing imperfections present in the aged copy. In rare cases, an imperfection in
the original, such as a blemish or missing page, may be replicated in our edition. We do,
however, repair the vast majority of imperfections successfully; any imperfections that
remain are intentionally left to preserve the state of such historical works.

Forgotten Books is a registered trademark of FB &c Ltd.
Copyright © 2015 FB &c Ltd.
FB &c Ltd, Dalton House, 60 Windsor Avenue, London, SW19 2RR.
Company number 08720141. Registered in England and Wales.

For support please visit www.forgottenbooks.com

1 MONTH OF
FREE
READING

at

www.ForgottenBooks.com

By purchasing this book you are
eligible for one month membership to
ForgottenBooks.com, giving you
unlimited access to our entire
collection of over 700,000 titles via
our web site and mobile apps.

To claim your free month visit:

www.forgottenbooks.com/free196519

* Offer is valid for 45 days from date of purchase. Terms and conditions apply.

Similar Books Are Available from
www.forgottenbooks.com

The Christian Mythology
by Brigham Leatherbee

Jesus and What He Said
by Arthur Salter Burrows

Reincarnation in the New Testament
by James Morgan Pryse

Dictionary of the Holy Bible
by William Wilberforce Rand

Being a Christian
by Jas A. Duncan

Heaven
by Dwight Lyman Moody

How to Pray
by R. A. Torrey

The Bible and Evolution
by W. H. Sparshott

The Aquarian Gospel of Jesus the Christ
by Levi

Christ and His Church in the Book of Psalms
by Andrew A. Bonar

Christian Healing
A Sermon Delivered at Boston, by Mary Baker Eddy

Church History Through All Ages
by Thomas Timpson

The Life of Jesus, Vol. 1 of 2
For the People, by David Friedrich Strauss

The Serpent, Satan and False Prophet
Or the Trinity of Evil, by Unknown Author

The Christian Faith and the Old Testament
by John M. Thomas

Christianity and Sex Problems
by Hugh Northcote

The Evolution of Spiritual Man
by William McIntire Lisle

The Beacon of Truth
Or Testimony of the Coran to the Truth of the Christian Religion, by William Muir

A Biblical View of the Church
by Josiah Goodman Bishop

Muhammad and Christ
by Moulvi Muhammad Ali

BIBLE TRIUMPHANT;

BEING

A REPLY TO A WORK

ENTITLED

144 SELF-CONTRADICTIONS of the BIBLE,

PUBLISHED BY ANDREW JACKSON DAVIS.

BY

Mrs. (H. V.) REED.

Elizabeth (Armstrong)

"As God is true, our word towards you was not yea and nay."—PAUL.

HARVARD, ILLINOIS:

PUBLISHED BY H. V. REED.

1866.

BS533
.B8 R4
1866

THOMAS G. NEWMAN   PRINTER.

HARVARD,   ILLINOIS.

PREFACE.

This work is presented to the public with the earnest hope that it may be productive of *good*. The pamphlet which is here reviewed, may appear to the thorough Bible student so weak as to need no reply. But through the channels of *Spiritualism* it has received a wide circulation, and several editions have been exhausted in poisoning the minds of casual readers against the truths of inspiration. It is considered the *strong tower* of skepticism and has been scattered over the land from Maine to California with the highest encomiums of the Infidel press. A contributor to the "*Herald of Progress*," thus writes: "Unless our judgment deceives us, the general reading of this work would oust from Christendom the last blind worshiper of the Bible, the contents of which are shown by this little *tell-tale*, to be a stupendous compound of contradiction and error. The most studious reader of the Bible will be *astonished* and *overwhelmed* at every step in going over these few pages to find how numerous and point-blank are the contradictions which fill the hitherto supposed God-given book." And the "*Liberator*," says: "It is an internal exhibition of the utter absurdity of the dogma of plenary inspiration, showing as it does at a glance, the multitudinous self-contradictions of the Bible, which no ingenuity of interpretation can reconcile, except that which can prove black to be white and white black." With such taunts as these the work has been thrown defiantly in the face of the christian world—and with a firm faith that "every word of God is pure," the defence has been undertaken, and so satisfactory are the evidences of the infallibility of God's word, that infidelity itself, *must* believe, if it would only investigate. In the prosecution of the work, various writers on sacred literature have been consulted, and I have endeavored to properly credit whatever information may have been derived therefrom. Valuable suggestions and criticisms have also been received from a few friends, whose services are hereby gratefully acknowledged. I have certainly endeavored to treat the compiler of the following propositions, with all *due* courtesy, and if some of my criticisms appear severe, be it remembered that they are prompted only by a keen sense of *justice*.

It is certainly a matter of congratulation to the christian world, to know that the man who has so insulted God, and violated his word, has enough self-respect *still*, to be ashamed to give his *name* to the public. Hence the compiler is unknown; consequently, the responsibility must rest upon the publisher, A. J. Davis.

To all who are honestly and fearlessly engaged in the investigation of Bible truth, and to those who are already sufficiently enlightened in the knowledge of God, to *appreciate* the glorious truths of His revelation, this little volume is affectionately dedicated, by

THE AUTHORESS.

THE BIBLE TRIUMPHANT.

THEOLOGICAL DOCTRINES.

1. God is satisfied with His Works.—And God saw everything that he had made, and behold it was very good. Gen. 1: 31.

God is Dissatisfied with His Works.—And it repented the Lord that he had made man on the earth, and it grieved him at his heart. Gen. 6: 6.

The above is the first specimen of the *so-called* "Self Contradictions of the Bible."— Gen. 1: 31, and Gen. 6: 6, are the first martyrs to be crucified upon the cross of modern skepticism. But we trust they can be rescued by a fair trial. Does it follow that because God was *satisfied* with the workmanship of his hand, in the morn of earth's creation, that he must be satisfied with all the sin and wickedness of man for 1500 years thereafter? The text in Gen. 1: 31 applies to the period *before* sin came into the world, when the whole physical creation was pure and lovely, and Gen. 6: 6 applies to the time when the earth was filled with wickedness and crime —when man stood in open defiance to God and his law. And so far as the Lord's *repenting* because He had made man is concerned, we would remark that *repentance* in the Bible means a "turning from a thing," and agreeable to this definition God turned from preserving man on the earth and destroyed him by the flood of waters, because of his sins against Him. Such repentance, God has shown in the overthrow of nations for their transgressions after having been sus-

tained by Him until they filled up their cup of
iniquity. Hence the *apparent* contradiction is
harmonized.

2. God dwells in Chosen Temples.—And the Lord appeared to
Solomon by night, and said unto him : I have heard thy prayer, and
have chosen this place to myself for a house of sacrifice...   For
now have I chosen and sanctified this house, that my name may be
there forever ; and mine eyes and my heart shall be there perpetual-
ly. 2 Chron. 7: 12. 16.

God dwells Not in Temples.—Howbeit the Most High dwelleth
not in temples made with hands, Acts 7: 48.

There is not even an *apparent* incongruity
here, for 2 Chron. 7: 12, 16, does not *intimate*
that the Jewish house of sacrifice was the place
of God's *residence* but simply as an *house of sacrifice*, and as having the *name* and approval of
God under the legal dispensation of Moses.   The
Queen of Brittain rules the province of the Cana-
das which is under her control but it does not
follow that she *resides* there. This, we think,
very aptly illustrates the above passage, and must
to every candid mind obviate the difficulty, if any
exists.   God made the temple at Jerusalem the
place of sacrifice, and He is represented as having his name and heart there continually, but the
presumption that therefore he must *personally*
dwell there, seems to betray more weakness of
discernment in our infidel compiler, than contradiction between the texts he has tried to
array against each other.

3. God dwells in Light.—Dwelling in light which no man can
approach unto. 1 Tim, 6: 18.

God dwells in Darkness.--The Lord said he would dwell in thick
darkness. 1 Kings 8: 12. He made darkness his secret place. Ps.
18: 11. Clouds and darkness are round about him. Ps. 97: 2,

The Lord *creates* both light and darkness, either

of which may be the dwelling-place of His power, and though light eternal surrounds His throne, may He not manifest his presence in the " thick darkness," or in the cloud of storm ? It may be said of man that he dwells in *light*, and then again he dwells in *darkness*, for each twenty-four hours presents these two conditions; and yet no one would infer that there must be a contradiction, because he thus alternately dwells in each. In like manner we may speak relatively of God, and say His dwelling place is amid the realms of eternal light, but when He manifests his power, makes " darkness pavillions round about him."— See 2 Sam. 22: 12. In order for the skeptic to sustain his position, he must show that God dwells *only* in light—then prove He dwells in darkness, but the Scripture will admit of no such construction, hence it does not contradict itself.

4. God is Seen and Heard.--And I will take away my hand and thou shalt *see* my back parts. Ex. 33: 23. And the Lord spake to Moses face to face, as a man speaketh to his friend. Ex. 33: 11. And the Lord called unto Adam, and said unto him, Where art thou?— And he said, I heard thy voice in the garden, and I was afraid.— Gen. 3: 9, 10. For I have seen God face to face, and my life is preserved. Gen. 32: 30. In the year that King Uzziah died, I saw, also, the Lord sitting upon a throne, high and lifted up. Isa. 6: 1. Then went up Moses and Aaron, Nadab and Abihu, and seventy of the elders of Israel. And they saw the God of Israel......... They saw God, and did eat and drink. Ex. 24: 9, 10, 11.

God is Invisible, and Cannot be Heard.--No man hath seen God at any time. John 1: 18 Ye have neither heard his voice, at any time, nor seen his shape. John 5: 37. And he said, Thou canst not see my face; for there shall no man see me and live. Ex. 33: 20.— Whom no man hath seen nor can see. 1 Tim. 6: 16.

If the words Lord and God in the passages above quoted, refer directly to the person of the Eternal Father, we are free to admit that the infidel has made out a *part* of his case, by finding one contradiction in the Bible. But if the texts referred to in the Old Testament speak of the angels of God and *not* of God himself, then all the discrepancy vanishes at once. We shall now show that the Lord seen and talked with "face to face" was not the Eternal, but his *angel* —the messenger of his will. The question will at once arise why the angel of God should be called Lord? The answer will appear from Ex. 23: 20, 21. " Behold I send an angel before thee ,, ., .. beware of him, and obey his voice, provoke him not, for he will not pardon your transgressions, for MY NAME IS IN HIM."— From this we learn that the angel of God bears His name. Hence the *Lord* that went before Israel, and was seen in the bush by Moses, and that Moses talked with " face to face" on Mount Sinai, was the *angel* sent forth from the presence of Jehovah. In proof of this, we refer the reader to Acts 7: 35–38. " This Moses they refused saying, Who made thee a ruler and a judge ? The same did God send to be a ruler and a deliverer, by the hand of his *angel* which appeared to him in the bush .....This is he that was in the church in the wilderness with the angel which spake, face to face, to him in the Mount Sinai, and with our fathers, who received the lively oracles to give unto us." From this it is clear that the *Lord* seen by Moses and the elders of Israel was the angel of Jehovah, and the same is true of the Lord seen face to face by Jacob, (Gen. 32: 30,) as the reader will learn by reading Hosea 12: 14. " Yea, he (Jacob) had power over the angel and prevailed." Here the Lord that wrestled with Jacob, is called by Hosea an angel, and by turning back to Gen. 32: 1, 2, it will be seen that angels appeared unto Jacob just before he beheld God face to face. " And Jacob went on his way and the angels of God met him, and when Jacob saw them, he said, This is God's host,"

&c. From the foregoing quotations we learn the following facts:

1. God put his *name* in the angel that he sent to do his will, and the angel performed his mission in the name of Him who sent him.

2. The appearances of the Lord, as recorded in the Old Testament are the appearances of the angel or angels of his presence, who did visibly appear and talk with men. Hence all the supposed discrepancy of the testimony on this point is obviated. The New Testament affirms that God (Greek ": *theos,*") has never been seen by man, which we believe is true, and the fact of the visible appearance of the angels to Moses and the fathers can never be made to oppose this great truth, or make the Bible appear contradictory.— There is another point which needs a remark, before dismissing this proposition. In Ex. 33: 11, it is stated that the Lord talked "face to face" with Moses, and in verse 20 the same angel says to him, "Thou canst not see my face, for there shall no man see me and live." We think, however, that a reconciliation may be fairly urged from the context. When the angel talked with Moses face to face, he did not appear *in his glory*, for after this, Moses entreats the angel talked with, saying, "I beseech thee show me thy glory." Verse 18. Now the angel, in whom dwelt the name of the Lord, assures him that he will cause all his goodness to pass before him, and that he will proclaim the name of the Lord ; and further informs him that he will place him in the clift of the rock and cause his glory to pass by, "but my face," says the angel, "shall not be seen." Hence Moses could have a *diminished* view of his glory. The solution, therefore, is apparent, the angel could not allow mortals to see his face, in his *glory* and *splendor*. The above reasoning will, we think, remove the cavil, and

1*

harmonize with the whole tenor of the chapter.—
The angel could be seen and talked with, as God's
messenger while disrobed of his glorious bright-
ness, but when clad in the splendors of Heaven,
mortals could not behold him and live. Hence the
skeptic again fails to make a discord in the testimony of Revelation. There are minor points in
the propositions reviewed above, but they are of
the same character of those already noticed, and
consequently need no reply at our hands.

5. God is Tired and Rests.--For in six days the Lord made
heaven and earth, and on the seventh day he *rested*, and was refreshed. Ex. 31: 17. I am weary with repenting. Jer. 15: 6..

God is Never tired, and Never Rests.--Hast thou not heard that
the everlasting God, the Lord, the Creator of the ends of the earth,
fainteth not, neither is *weary*. Isa. 40: 28.

The effort here made is purely of a technical
character, and will need but a few words to expose the infidel's cavil.

In regard to God's *resting* and being *refreshed*,
we would say that the Douay Bible gives us a fair
translation of the passage, "For in six days the
Lord made heaven and earth, and in the seventh
day he *ceased* from work." This view of the text
at once removes all objections. Jer. 15: 6, " I
am *weary* of repenting," does not express the idea
of *physical exhaustion* on the part of God, but a
state of regret for the many sins of his people
whereas Isa. 40: 28 implies that God has *ability*
to perform *without* exhausting his power.

The one text (Jer. 15: 6,) alludes to God's
sympathy with his people, and his sorrow for their
disobedience, while the other shows that he is
able to execute all he has promised. Hence the
texts are not contradictory.

6. God is Everywhere Present, Sees and Knows all Things.
The eyes of the Lord are in every place. Prov. 15: 3. Whither shall

I flee from thy presence? If I ascend up into heaven, thou art there; if I make my bed in hell, behold, thou art there. If I take the wings of the morning, and dwell in the uttermost parts of the earth even there shall thy hand lead me, and thy right hand hold me. Ps. 139: 7, 10. There is no darkness nor shadow of death, where the workers of iniquity may hide themselves. For his eyes are upon the ways of man, and he seeth all his goings. Job 34: 22, 21.

God is Not everywhere present, Neither sees nor knows all things.—And the Lord *came down to see* the city and the town, Gen. 11: 5. And the Lord said, Because the cry of Sodom and Gomorrah is great, and because their sin is very grievous, I will *go down* now and *see* whether they have done altogether according to the cry of it, which is come unto me; and *if not*, I will know. Gen, 18: 20, 21.—And Adam and his wife *hid* themselves from the presence of the Lord, amongst the trees of the garden. Gen, 3: 8.

The Omniscience of God is a plain doctrine of Revelation, and to suppose otherwise is to undeify him, and rob him of his divinity. The skeptic, however claims that the Bible is inharmonious on this point, inasmuch as it teaches that God is not all-wise, and as proof we are referred to Gen. 11: 5, Gen. 18: 20, 21, Gen. 3: 8. The most important of which we will examine. Gen. 18, 20, 21 may be considered the most worthy of notice. The Lord here spoken of as coming down to see if the cities were as sinful as was reported, &c., has reference to the ANGELS who came down from Heaven to inflict judgment upon these wicked cities, provided that a certain number of righteous men could not be found therein. This position will appear plain by examining the context, and will, we trust, remove the obscurity. In Gen. 18: 1, it is stated that "the Lord appeared" unto Abraham, the second verse says Abraham saw "three men," and in the third verse he addresses them as "my Lord." Two of these angels journey towards Sodom while one remains, and with him Abraham pleads for the saving of the city.— The two angels appear in Sodom at even, (Gen. 12: 1,) and Lot addresses them as "My Lords," and in verse thirteen they make known to Lot their mission in these words, "For we will destroy this place, because the cry of them is waxen great before the face of the Lord, and the Lord hath *sent us* to destroy it," see also verses 15 and 16.   Hence the Lord here spoken of had direct reference to the angels of God who came down from Heaven to execute the judgment of Jehovah.

7. *God knows the Hearts of Men.*—Thou, Lord, which knowest the hearts of men., Acts 1: 24. Thou knowest my down-sitting and mine up-rising ; thou understandest my thought afar off. Thou compassest my path and my lying down, and art acquainted with all my ways. Ps. 139: 2, 3.

God tries Men to find out what is in their Hearts.—The Lord your God, proveth you, to *know* whether ye love the Lord, your God with all your heart and with all your soul. Deut. 13: 3. The Lord thy God led thee these forty years in the wilderness, to humble thee, and to prove thee, to *know* what was in thy heart. Deut. 8; 2. For now I know that thou fearest God, seeing that thou hast not withheld thy son, thine only son, from me. Gen. 22: 12.

This proposition does not *indicate* a contradiction, neither has the infidel compiler so stated it as to make it *appear* incongruous.   For God may *know* the hearts of all men, which is the truth, and he may wish to *try* them, not indeed to satisfy himself, but to make examples of his people in order to prove to the world the *certainty* of truth, and to show his faithfulness in all his promises ; we shall therefore dismiss this without further notice.

8.   *God is All-powerful.*—Behold, I am the Lord, the God of all flesh ; is there anything too hard for me? Jer. 32: 27. With God *all* things are possible. Matt. 19: 26,

God is Not All-powerful.—And the Lord was with Judah, and he drove out the inhabitants of the mountain ; but *could not drive out* the inhabitants of the valley, because they had chariots of iron.— **Judg.** 1: 19.

That God is Omnipotent, we most heartily believe, and that he is *able* to fulfill *all* he has spoken, we claim to be the basis of all true faith.— But the skeptic brings forward Judg. 1: 19, to prove that God was so deficient in power that he could not even drive out the inhabitants of the valley because they had "iron chariots;" but a grammatical examination of the text will show that the antecedent of the pronoun "*he*," is *not* Jehovah, but *Judah.* It does not follow that because the Lord assisted Judah under many circumstances, that therefore he would be with Judah in *all* his undertakings. It was therefore *Judah*, not Jehovah, who could not drive them out of the valley in consequence of their iron chariots. The Douay· Bible translates it much plainer than King James' version. It reads as follows: " And the Lord was with Judah, and he (Judah) possessed the hill country, but was not able to destroy the inhabitants of the valley, because they had many chariots armed with scythes."

The above leaves no room for doubt, for the same one who *possessed the hill country* was the one that failed to obtain the valley, and it is clear that this was Judah:

9. *God is Unchangeable.*—With whom is *no* variableness, neither shadow of turning. Jam. 1: 17. For I am the Lord; I change not. Mal. 3: 6. I, the Lord, have spoken it ; it shall come to pass and I will do it. I will not go back, neither will I spare, neither will I repent. Ezek. 24: 14. God is *not* a man that he should lie neither the son of man that he should *repent.* Num. 23: 19.

***God is Changeable.*—**And it *repented* the Lord that he had made man on the earth, and it grieved him at his heart. Gen. 6: 6. And God saw their works, that they turned from their evil way ; and God *repented* of the evil that he had said he would do unto them, and he did it not. Jonah 3:10. Wherefore the Lord God of Israel saith, I said, indeed, that thy house, and the house of thy father, should walk before me forever ; but now the Lord saith, Be it far from me .... Behold, the days come that I will cut off thine arm, and the arm of thy father's house. 1 Sam. 2: 30, 31. In those days was Hezekiah sick unto death. And the prophet Isaiah. the son of Amoz, came unto him, and said unto him, Thus saith the Lord, set thy house in order; for thou shalt die, and not live.........And it came to pass afore Isaiah was gone out into the middle court, that the word of the Lord came unto him, saying, Turn again and tell Hezekiah, the captain of my people, thus saith the Lord,......... I have heard thy prayer,......... and I will add unto thy days, fifteen years. 2 Kings 20; 1, 4-6. And the Lord said unto Moses, Depart and go up hence· thou and the people......... For I will *not go up* in the midst of thee' ....And the Lord said, I will do this thing, also, that thou hast spoken.........My presence *shall go with thee*, and I will give thee rest. Ex. 33: 1, 3, 17, 14.

God has stated in the Scriptures his purpose in regard to some things, concerning which he will never repent or change. his course of action, among these we may mention Num. 23: 19. Balak tried to get Balaam to curse Israel, but the prophet each time blessed Jacob instead of cursing him, and at last he assured Balak that God *would not* repent, or turn from blessing Israel.— Hence Balak failed in his endeavor to have the Lord turn from and act in opposition to his word.

On the other hand there *are* things of which God promises to repent, if the people confess their sins and turn to him. For he declared by the mouth of Jeremiah, that "If that nation against whom I have pronounced, turn from their evil way, I *will* repent of, or turn from the evil I thought to do unto them " Jer. 18: 8. And this was fulfilled when the people of Nineveh turned from their sins, for God then repented of the evil he had pronounced against them and did it not. But this by no means proves that the Bible contradicts itself. God repented that he had made man, that is he turned from preserving him upon the earth and destroyed him by the flood of waters. We might notice other points in the above proposition, but we trust that the reader will at once see the principle on which they all harmonize. God or man may make promises which they will not repent of, or turn from, and again they may promise certain things *on conditions*, and yet no one would accuse them of inconsistency in this respect. If the reader will examine the above texts in their connection, he will see that the compiler of the little work before us has totally ignored the principles of reason and justice.

10. God is Just and Impartial.—The Lord is upright,...... and there is no unrighteousness in him. Ps.92: 15. Shall not the Judge of all the earth do right ? Gen.18: 25. A God of truth, and without iniquity, *just* and *right* is he. Deut. 32: 4. There is no respect of persons with God. Rom. 2: 11. Ye say the way of the Lord is not equal. Hear now, O house of Israel; is not my way equal? Ezek. 18: 25.

God is Unjust and Partial.--Cursed be Canaan ; a servant of servants shall he be unto his brethren. Gen. 9: 25. For I, the Lord thy God, am a jealous God, visiting the iniquity of the fathers upon the children unto the third and fourth generations. Exo. 20: 5. For the children being not yet born, neither having done any good or evil, that the purpose of God, according to election, might stand, ... it was said unto her, The elder shall serve the younger. As it is written, Jacob have I *loved*, and Esau have I *hated*. Rom 11: 12, 13. For whosoever hath, to him shall be given, and he shall have more abundance; but whosoever hath not, from him shall be taken away even that he hath. Matt· 13: 12.

It is true that God is upright and holy, and that he is just and righteous. It is also true that with Him "there is no respect of persons," but he has respect for character and goodness. As to the curse which fell upon Canaan, it was a prophecy of the *woe* which would follow the sinful conduct of the Canaanites as a *nation*, for the curse never fell on Canaan personally. This prophecy did not *create* the servitude of the nation, but simply *foretold* what would come to pass in the future, and it was literally fulfilled. Exo. 20: 5, shows that God is jealous for the welfare of his people, and also that fathers and children who practice *ini-*

quity, will alike meet with judgments from the hand of God. The text does not teach that the fathers do all the sinning and escape judgment, while the children do NOT sin and still receive the punishment due their fathers. The idea of the text is, that fathers and children would *all* be punished for practicing iniquity. The reference to Jacob and Esau is purely *national*, meaning the two people, or their descendants—one doing the will of God, and the other disobeying his word. In proof that the reference is national, and not individual, please read Gen. 25: 22–23.

We now ask the reader in the light of the foregoing facts, if the skeptic has sustained his proposition that God is unjust or unrighteous? We think there is no way of making the Bible appear at variance with itself, except by thus wresting a few sentences from their proper connection, and a few words of explanation will at all times expose the infidels' hatred for God's word.

11. *God is the Author of Evil.*—Out of the mouth of the Most High proceedeth not evil and good ? Lam. 3: 38. Thus saith the Lord, Behold I *frame* evil against you and devise a device against **you.**—Jer. 18: 11. I make peace and *create evil*: I the Lord do all these things. Isa. 45: 7. Shall there be evil in the city, and the Lord hath not done it ? Amos 3: 6. Wherefore I gave them also statutes that were not good, and judgments whereby they should not live.—Ezek. 20: 25.

God is Not the Author of Evil.—God is not the author of confusion. 1 Cor. 14. 33. A God of truth and without iniquity, *just* and *right* is he. Deut. 32: 4. For God cannot be tempted with evil, neither tempteth he any man, Jas. 1: 13.

The word *evil* has two meanings in the Bible. It means *punishment,* and also *sin.* When it says that God creates evil, it merely conveys the idea that he executes judgments. When it states that *man* does evil, it is a record of his sins against God. This will be plainly seen by read-

ing 1 Kings 16: 25, 30. Job 2: 10. Isa. 45: 7.—
(See Cruden.)

We conclude on this point, therefore, that
though God inflicts *evil* upon the wicked for their
sins, still the Judge of all the earth will do right.

12. ***God gives Freely to those who Ask.***--If any of you lack
wisdom, let him ask of God, that *giveth to all men freely* and up-
braideth not, and it shall be given unto him. James 1: 5. For every
one that asketh receiveth and he that seeketh findeth. Luke 11: 10.

***God Withholds His Blessings and Prevents Men from Receiv-
ing Them.***--He hath blinded their eyes and hardened their hearts
that they should not see with their eyes, nor understand with their
hearts, and be converted, and I should heal them. John 12: 40. For
it was of the Lord to *harden their hearts*, that they should come
against Israel in battle, that he might destroy them utterly, and that
they might have no favor, Josh 11: 20. O Lord, why hast thou
made us to err from thy ways and *hardened* our heart? Isa. 63: 17.

That God gives freely to those who ask of him,
is true, providing they do not " ask amiss ;" then
they receive *not.*

The infidel wishes to make it appear in opposition to the above position, that God intentionally
blinded the eyes of the Jewish nation, lest they
should embrace Christ, and refers to John 12: 40,
as proof. This however fails him, for it does not
happen to be a decree that the Jews *must* reject
Christ, but a prophecy of Isaiah's showing that
they *would* reject him. Hence the passage is altogether misapplied. See Matt. 13: 14.

The reference to Josh. 11: 20, is to those wicked nations that fought against Israel, and the
Lord overthrew them for their hatred to his
cause and to his people. Isa. 63: 17, and its connection shows that Israel had *forsaken* God, and
when they pleaded for forgivness, he returned to
them in the plentitude of his mercy. These texts
therefore, cannot be forced to antagonize other
parts of God's word.

13. God is to be Found by those who Seek Him.--Every one that asketh receiveth, and he that seeketh findeth. Matt. 7: 8.--Those that seek me early shall find me. Prov. 8: 17.

God is Not to be Found by those Who Seek Him.--Then shall they call upon me but I will *not* answer ; they shall seek me early but shall *not* find me. Prov, 1: 28.

Matt. 7: 8, and Prov. 8: 17, refer to the period of offered mercy. Whereas, Prov. 1: 28, refers to the time after mercy ceases to be offered and judgment about to be executed. This will be seen by reading the verses preceding and following. " When your fear cometh as desolation, and your destruction cometh as a whirlwind ; when distress and anguish cometh upon you, Then shall they call upon me but I will not answer; They shall seek me early but they shall not find me ; for that they hated knowledge and did not choose the fear of the Lord." Prov. 1: 27-29. The connection cited above, relieves the text from all obscurity, and takes the objection from the over-anxious infidel.

14. God is Warlike.--The Lord is a man of *war*. Exo. 15: 3.--The Lord of *Hosts* is his name. Isa. 51: 25.

God is Peaceful.--The God of *peace*. Rom. 15: 33. God is not the author of confusion but of *peace*. 1 Cor. 14: 33

The Lord is a man of *war* to all his enemies, and a God of *peace* to all who obey him. He is a God of *wrath* to his foes, and of *goodness* to his children. Were it not that the skeptic was determined to find just 144 contradictions of the Bible, he would never have inserted the above

15. God is Cruel, Unmerciful, Destructive and Ferocious.--I will *not pity* nor *spare*, nor have *mercy*, but *destroy*. Jer. 13: 14. And thou shalt consume all the people which the Lord thy God shall de-. liver thee ; thine eye shall have no pity upon them. Deut. 7: 16 Now go and smite Amalek, and utterly *destroy* all that they have, and spare them not, but *slay* both man and woman, infant and suckling. 1 Sam. 15: 2, 3. Because they had looked into the ark of the Lord, even he smote of the people fifty thousand, and three score and ten men. 1 Sam. 6: 19. The Lord thy God is a consuming fire. Deut. 4: 24.

God is Kind, Merciful and Good. The Lord is very pitiful and of tender *mercy.* Jam. 5: 11. For he doth not afflict willingly, nor grieve the children of men. Lam. 3: 33. For his mercy endureth forever. 1 Chron. 16: 34. I have no *pleasure* in the death of him that dieth, saith the Lord God. Ezek. 18: 32. The Lord is *good to all,* and his tender mercies are over *all* his works. Ps. 145: 9. Who will have all men to be saved, and to come unto the knowledge of the truth. 1 Tim. 2: 4. God is *love.* 1 John 4: 16. Good and upright is the Lord. Ps. 25: 8.

It has ever been the boast of Infidel writers, that the God of the Bible is cruel and unmerciful, and the texts brought forth in the first part of the above proposition, are ever quoted to sustain this idea. If the reader will take the trouble to examine the passages referred to, in their connection, he will see that they *all* allude to the judgments of God falling upon wicked nations, for their sins against him. In Jer. 13: 14, God proposes to destroy the nation of Israel from the land, because they had sinned with a high hand, and trampled on his holy law, but before the threatened judgment was executed, he offered them pardon and forgiveness if they would turn unto Him and cease to pervert his ways. Hence this text is purely of a judicial character, and cannot be made to sustain the skeptic's attack. Deut. 7: 16, alludes to those nations that were vindictive enemies to God's people, and he commanded Israel to destroy them. This also was a judgment visited upon the sinful, and therefore founded in justice. The same is true of 1 Sam. 15: 2, 3.— Amalek had done much evil to the people of Israel when they were in the wilderness, killing those that lingered behind in their march, that were fatigued and weary, &c. And for these acts of hostility, God had decreed the overthrow of the Amalekites, and the time now came for its execution. But why, it will be asked, did God decree the destruction of women and helpless infants? We answer, it was a judgment upon a nation, and as such it fell upon *all*. It was so in the days of the flood, and so of Sodom and Gomorrah. Indeed, the infidel who blames the "God of the Bible," and boasts of his "God of Nature," is in a worse difficulty than this, for his God buries millions by earthquakes and volcanoes, many of whom are innocent women and helpless babes. His acts are not deserved judgments for sin, but they come without warning or mercy, upon the innocent and helpless. But, says the infidel, they transgressed a *physical* law, and must suffer its penalty. So we say of those nations. They transgressed a *moral* law, and they suffered its penalty. The infidel sees no cruelty in his "God of Nature" visiting families by disease, by famine and pestilence, taking all the little ones from affectionate parents; he sees no injustice in his "God of Nature," in executing the penalty of violated law. Yet if the God of the Bible inflicts a judgment upon a nation of sinners, he is frightened, and exclaims *cruelty!! unmerciful! ferocious!!!* Reader be not deceived. It is done to lead you from the God of truth, who does all things for the best, for the good of man, and for His own glory.

16. *God's Anger is Fierce and Endures Long.*—And the Lord's *anger* was kindled against Israel, and he made them wander in the wilderness *forty years* until all the generation that had done evil in the sight of the Lord was consumed. Num. 32: 13. And the Lord said unto Moses, Take all the heads of the people and hang them up before the Lord against the sun, that the *fierce anger* of the the Lord may be turned away from Israel. Num. 25: 4, For I have kindled a fire in mine *anger* which shall burn *forever.* Jer. 17: 4.

God's Anger is Slow and Endures but for a Moment.—The Lord is merciful and gracious, *slow to anger* and plentious in mercy. Ps. 193: 8, His anger *endureth but a moment.* Ps. 30: 5.

Num. 32: 13, is-cited, to convey the idea that the Lord's anger against Israel continued for forty years. But the words of the text only imply that they were made to wander in the wilderness forty years, because of their sins against Jehovah. It marks the duration of the *punishment*, instead of God's anger. He was angry with them for their sins, and pronounced upon their guilty heads the decree of punishment, but no rational man would therefore conclude that God's *anger* lasted until His decree was fulfilled. Num. 25: 4, simply speaks of the "fierce anger" of Jehovah, without reference to its duration. There is surely no inconsistency here. God is "slow to anger, and plenteous in mercy," but when his wrath is kindled by man's rebellion, it may be "fierce," although it "endureth but a moment." Jer. 17: 4, is a MIS-QUOTATION. The Bible reads, "For YE have kindled a fire in mine anger which shall burn forever." Even our infidel compiler must admit that this correction makes a "material" change in the idea. He must either be very careless or very dishonest, who conveys the idea that it was GOD who kindled the fire. Our correction removes all obscurity from the text; for no grammarian can for a moment suppose that it is God's anger which is to burn forever, when the Word so plainly states that it is the fire which JUDAH had kindled.

**17. *God Commands, Approves of, and Delights in Burnt Offerings, Sacrifices, and Holy Days.*—Thou shalt offer every day a bullock for a sin offering for atonement. Ex. 29: 36. On the tenth day of this seventh month, there shall be a day of atonement . it shall be a holy convocation unto you, and ye shall afflict your souls and offer an offering made by fire unto the Lord. Lev. 23: 27. And thou shalt burn the whole ram upon the altar ;......... it is a *sweet savor*; an offering made by fire unto the Lord. Ex. 29: 18.— And the priest shall burn it all on the altar to be a burnt sacrifice, an offering made by fire, of a *sweet savor* unto the Lord. Lev. 1: 9.

God Disapproves of, and has no pleasure in them.—For I *spake not* unto your fathers, nor commanded them in the day that I brought them out of the land of Egypt, concerning burnt offerings or sacrifices. Jer. 7: 22. Your burnt offerings are *not* acceptable, *nor* your sacrifices sweet unto me. Jer. 6: 20. Will I eat of the flesh of bulls, or drink the blood of goats? Offer unto God thanksgiving, and pay thy vows unto the Most High. Ps. 50: 13, 14. Bring no more vain oblations; incense is an abomination unto me; the new moons and sabbaths, the calling of assemblies I cannot away with; it is iniquity, even the solemn meeting......... To what purpose is the multitude of your sacrifices unto me? saith the Lord. I am full of the burnt offerings of rams, and the fat of fed beasts, and I *delight not* in the blood of bullocks, or of lambs, or of he goats. When ye come to appear before me, who hath required this at your hand. Isa. 1: 13, 11, 12.

Under the dispensation of the *law*, God commanded and approved of sacrifices and burnt offerings, but there was a time when the Jews depended *alone* upon burnt offerings to find favor with God, while they neglected and even despised his other requirements. Hence, in Jer. 7: 22, we find a strong *idiom* of the original Hebrew which does not show that God holds sacrifices in contempt, but that there are *other things* which he appreciates more highly; the true elipsis of the text expressed in our tongue is the following: "For I spake not unto your Fathers, nor commanded them (*alone*)... concerning burnt offerings and sacrifices." This idea is fully explained by the following verse, But this thing commanded I them saying, Obey my voice (in all things, not merely in relation to burnt offerings) and I will be your God and ye shall be my people; and walk ye in ALL the ways that I have commanded that it may be well unto you." See 1 Sam. 15: 22, "Behold to *obey* is *better* than sacrifice, and to hearken than the fat of rams."

Ps. 50: 13, 14, expresses the same idea, viz:— That *thanksgiving* and the *fulfillment* of their vows were more acceptable to the Lord of hosts than even the burnt offerings of the Mosaic dispensation. Jer. 6: 20, and Isa. 1: 13, 11: 12, are fully explained by the context. It is the refusal of Jehovah to accept offerings from those who had rebelled and gone far from His commands. These are the. declarations of the Most High that sacrifices are *not* acceptable from those who continually work iniquity. Had the skeptic read the *whole* of the two chapters, he has here quoted from, he could not *honestly* have cited these texts as contradictions of God's law.

18. God Accepts Human Sacrifices.—The king (David) took the two sons of Rizpah,..........and the five sons of Michal ;..........and he delivered them into the hands of the Gibeonites, and they hanged them in the hill *before the Lord*......... And after that God was entreated for the land. 2 Sam, 21: 8, 9, 14. And he (God) said, Take now thy son, thine only son Isaac whom thou lovest, and get thee into the land of Moriah, and *offer* him there for a *burnt offering.* Gen. 22: 2. And Jephthah vowed a *vow* unto the Lord, and said, If thou shalt without fail deliver the children of Ammon into my hands, then it shall be that whosoever cometh forth ot the doors of my house to meet me when I return in peace from the children of Ammon, shall surely be the Lord's, and I will offer it up for a *burnt offering.* So Jephthah passed over unto the children of Ammon to fight against them; and the Lord delivered them into his hands......... And Jephthah came to Mizpeh unto his house and behold, his daughter came out to meet him......... And he sent her away for two months; and she went with her companions and bewailed her virginity upon the mountains. And it came to pass at the end of two months that she returned unto her father, who *did* according to his *vow* which he had made. Judges 11: 30, 31, 32, 34, 38, 39.

God Forbids Human Sacrifice.—Take heed to thyself that thou be not snared by following them [the Gentile nations;].... for every abomination to the Lord which he hateth have they done unto their gods; for even their sons and their daughters have they *burnt* in the *fire* to *their gods.* Deut. 12: 30, 31.

The enemy of the Bible can produce no evidence that the act of David recorded in 2 Sam. 21, (and which the context greatly mitigates,) or the rashness of Jephthah, was acceptable to God. Why does he *assume* that which he must know he cannot prove? That he should quote Gen. 22: 2 to sustain his proposition betrays more weakness than we expected to find, even in the ranks of skepticism. Has he never read the touching history of Abraham and Isaac—or does he suppose his readers to be ignorant of the patriarchs' trial, and the glorious triumph of his faith on the sacred brow of Mount Moriah? It is a golden record of the love of that God who pitieth them that fear him, "as a father pitieth his children." Truely the God of Heaven "forbids human sacrifice."

19. God Tempts Men.—And it came to pass, that God *did tempt* Abraham, Gen. 22: 1. And again the anger of the Lord was kindled against Israel, and he moved David against them to say, Go number Israel and Judah. 2 Sam, 24: 1. O Lord, thou hast *deceived* (marginal reading, *enticed*) me, and I was deceived (enticed.) Jer. 20: 7. Lead us not into temptation. Matt. 6: 13.

God Tempts No Man.—Let no man say when he is tempted, I am tempted of God ; for God cannot be tempted with evil, *neither tempteth he any man.* James 1: 13.

In Gen. 22: 1, it declares that "God did tempt Abraham." It is the preface to the history of God's *trial* of his faithful servant, and the word which is translated *tempt* is the Hebrew word "*nah-sah,*" and the literal rendering of it is, "to try, to prove any one,—to put him to the test," (see "Gesenius' Hebrew Lexicon," page 676.)— Hence God TESTED Abraham, and the patriarch's faith was proved to be as bright as molten gold. The fiery trial only served to purify and strengthen his faith in the living God, and the record still burns upon the sacred page in all its ancient beauty—a glorious example for God's children in all ages.

The next text under consideration is 2 Sam. 24: 1, and this is GROSSLY MISREPRESENTED, the Bible reads," and *he* (*Satan,* see margin,) moved

David," so it was *Satan* and not Jehovah that moved David to number Israel. Cannot the skeptic see the difference?

The word rendered "deceived or enticed" in Jer. 20: 7, is "*pah-tha*," which Gesenius defines thus, "to persuade any one," and refers to this very text as an illustration of the term. Hence the passage in question might be literally rendered "Thou hast persuaded me, and I was enticed, (see Gesenius, page 875.) The text "Lead us not into temptation" is thus translated by McKnight, "Abandon us not to temptation." And this surely gives a correct idea of the verse in question. Hence we repeat, "Let no man say when he is tempted, I am tempted of God."

20. God Cannot Lie.—It is impossible for God to *lie*. Heb. 6: 18.

God Lies by Proxy; He sends forth Lying Spirits to Deceive.—For this cause God shall send them strong delusion, that they should believe a *lie.* 2 Thess. 2: 11. Now, therefore, behold, the Lord hath *put a lying spirit* in the mouth of all these thy prophets, and the Lord hath spoken evil concerning thee. 1 Kings 23: 22,— And if the prophet be deceived when he hath spoken a thing, I the Lord have deceived that prophet. Ezek. 14: 9.

None of the texts quoted above implicate God in a falsehood.

The facts are, that God *permitted* certain things to be done, which resulted in Judgments upon the sinful. He *permits* strong delusion to come upon those who reject his truth, as in 2 Thess. 2: 11. And in the case of the King who would not believe God's prophets, we find that lying spirits were allowed to fill the mouths of the prophets of Ahab. Not indeed that God sanctioned lying, but as Ahab had rejected his truth, and would not receive His prophets, therefore lying spirits were *permitted* to lead him on to certain destruction. It must however be borne in mind that from the 19th verse to the 24th, is a a recital of a *vision* of the prophet, and not by any means to be understood literally. It is true that God is represented in the Bible as *doing* things, which he only *permits*, this however, is common to Scripture phraseology. " In Matt. 8: 32, the Lord Jesus is represented as commanding the devils to *go* into the herd of swine "and he said unto them GO." Now if we consult the preceding verse we will perceive that the devils had first actually " besought him;" therefore the expression GO was used merely to signify his compliance with their urgent request, and therefore, was used purely *permissively*." See Dr. Sleigh's Def. Dic.

21. *Because of Man's Wickedness God Destroys Him.*

And God saw that the *wickedness* of man was *great* in the earth, and that every imagination of the thoughts of his heart was only evil continually........., And the Lord said, I will *destroy* man whom I have created. Gen. 6: 5, 7.

Because of Man's Wickedness God will Not destroy him.— And the Lord said in his heart, I *will not* again curse the ground any more for man's sake; for the imagination of man's heart is evil from his youth ; neither will I smite any more every living thing.— Gen. 8: 21.

There is not even a *semblance* of error here, for Gen. 6: 5, 7 shows that God will destroy the wicked. But Gen. 8: 21 is a promise that God will curse the ground no more, nor destroy every living thing. This does not say, however, that he will no more destroy the wicked, for he could easily destroy the sinners of earth without destroying every living thing. Skeptics should be more careful and not *wrest* the Scriptures, nor contradict their own ideas of language and good sense, for they claim to be models of consistency.

22. *God's Attributes are Revealed in His Works.*—For the

invisible things of him from the creation of the world are clearly seen, being understood by the things that are made, even his eternal power and Godhead. Rom. 1: 20.

God's Attributes Cannot be Discovered.—Canst thou by searching find out God? Job 11: 7. There is no searching his understanding. Isa. 40: 28.

Were it not that this proposition is in the series, we should pass it by without comment, for it certainly needs charity to even think the infidel *candid* in the above quotations. The Apostle in Rom. 1: 20 is showing that a knowledge of God's existence and providence can be clearly learned by the physical creation, or as the Psalmist says, "The heavens declare the glory of God—the firmament showeth his handywork."—Psa. 19: 1. The whole Universe proclaims a God, infinite in power, wisdom and righteousness. But with this display of His glory and majesty we cannot find Him out to perfection, and if the skeptic had quoted the whole verse in Job 11: 7, he would have answered his own cavil. We will here quote it, so that the reader can see how beautifully the Bible explains itself: "Canst thou, by searching, find out God? Canst thou find out the Almighty unto PERFECTION?" This at once takes from the infidel the apparent discrepancy which was made by garbling Job 11: 7. Nothing can ever be gained by misrepresenting ANY author, unless it is a *bad* reputation.

23. *There is but One God.*—The Lord our God is *one* Lord.—Deut. 6: 4.

There is a Plurality of Gods.—And God said, Let *us* make man in *our* image. Gen, 1: 26. And the Lord God said, Behold the man is become as one of *us*. Gen. 1: 26. And the Lord appeared unto him (Abraham) in the plains of Mamre......... And he lifted up his eyes and looked, and lo, *three* men stood by him; and when he saw them he ran to meet them from the tent door, and bowed himself toward the ground, and said, My Lord, if now I have found favor in thy sight, pass not away, I pray thee, from they servant. Gen. 18: 1, 2, 3. For there are *three* that bear record in Heaven, the Father, the Word, and the Holy Ghost. 1 John 5: 7.

The *one-ness* of the Eternal Father is every-where taught in the Holy Writings. Truly we can say our God is one. But this by no means implies that the word *God* always means the same Eternal Spirit. It is applied to idols and to men in many places in the Holy Scriptures, as the reader will see by examining a Concordance.—The word *God* also is applied to the His angels. In Gen. 1: 26 it is said: "And *God* said, let *us* make man in *our* image." The word here trans-lated *God*, is, in the Hebrew, "Elohim," and is the same word translated gods in Gen. 3: 5.

The word Elohim is plural, and is applied to the angels of the Eternal Spirit, who bear the name of Him who sent them.

In order to satisfy the reader that the above is true, we will give one case in point. In Psa. 97: 7, it is said of Christ, "Worship Him, all ye gods." And Paul in quoting this text in Hebrews 1: 6 * gives it thus: "Let all the angels of God worship Him." Hence, Gen. 1: 26, where the plural form is used, applies to God's angels, who came to do his will in the creation of man. The Deity can, at pleasure, empower his angels to perform His will, and what He does, by or through them, he does himself. After man sinned, the "Elohim" says, "the man has become as one of us, to know good and evil."—Hence all these plural forms of the pronouns find their solution in the word "Elohim," which is also plural, and in many cases they have also the verbs agreeing with them in numbers. We can-not believe that the Deity *personally* came to earth, and performed all the acts ascribed to Him.

But as we have before seen, the Deity has put his name in the angels who do his will on earth. This position is fairly illustrated in Gen. 18: 1,

---

* Barnes' Notes on Hebrews 1 : 6.

2, 3, which the skeptic quotes above to falsify the Bible, but which in reality tends to harmonize its difficulties. In this case the three angels which meet Abraham, he calls "My Lord." Hence this very text takes from the infidel his chief weapon of attack. So far as 1 John 5: 7 is concerned, we would remark that the three which bear record in heaven are, the *Father*, who is the one Deity, and the *Word* which was made flesh by the Deity, and dwelt among men; and the Holy Spirit which proceeds forth from the (one) Father and the (one) Son. And as to the three being *one*, we would say, they are one as far as the bearing of the record is concerned, (as the sense of the text implies,) but not "one God," which would ignore the sense of Divine Revelation. We therefore conclude that these passages are fairly explained by the Scriptures themselves; and had the compiler of "Self-Contradictions" been as zealous in learning the Scriptures as he has been in trying to find discrepancies in them, he would not now be found fighting against God.

We now dismiss chap. 1st and appeal to the candor and good sense of the reader to decide whether there is ONE proposition fairly sustained by the infidel who wishes to destroy confidence in the blessed Bible, so that he may sow rank weeds of a heartless and unholy philosophy in the minds of men. May the God of the Bible smile upon the writer and reader, and may his truth lead us into the Way of Life and the glories of Eternity.

24. *Robbery Commanded.*—When ye go, ye shall not go empty; but every woman shall *borrow* of her neighbor, and of her that sojourneth in her house, jewels of silver, and jewels of gold, and raiment: and ye shall put them upon your sons, and upon your daughters: and ye shall *spoil* the Egyptians. Ex. 3: 21, 22. And they borrowed of the Egyptians jewels of silver, and jewels of gold, and raiment.........And they spoiled the Egyptians, Ex. 12: 35, 36.

Robbery Forbidden.—Thou shalt *not* defraud thy neighbor, neither *rob* him. Lev. 19: 13. Thou shalt *not* steal. Ex. 20: 15.

Infidels in every age of the world have taken advantage of the fact that God commanded the Israelites to carry with them, when they left the land, a part of the wealth which *nominally* belonged to the Egyptians. Cannot even a skeptic see the justice of this? Has he never read of the long years during which Israel toiled without recompense? Has he never heard of the wealth which they amassed for their Egyptian masters? Or *why* does he accuse the God of Heaven, of injustice, when he commands Israel to take a *small portion* of their *own earnings.* Truly "thou shalt not defraud thy neighbor;" but Israel had been defrauded for ages, and because Israel's God takes from the Egyptians a portion of their ill-gotten spoils, and returns it to those who *earned* it,—those weak and puny men who *dare* to sit in judgment upon the acts of Jehovah, have set up the cry of "Robbery!" Oh! humanity, where is thy shame?

25. *Lying Approved and Sanctioned.* — And the woman (Rahab) took the two men and hid them and said thus: There came men unto me, but I wist not whence they were: and it came to pass about the time of shutting of the gate, when it was dark, that the men went out; whither the men went I wot not; pursue after them quickly, for ye shall overtake them. But she had brought them up to the roof of the house and hid them with the stalks of flax, Josh. 2: 4, 5. 6. Was not Rahab the harlot *justified* by works, when she had received the messengers, and had sent them out another way ? James 2: 25. And the king of Egypt called for the mid-wives, and said unto them, Why have ye done this thing, and have saved the men-children alive ? And the midwives said unto Pharaoh, Because the Hebrew women are not as the Egyptian women : for they are lively, and are delivered ere the midwives come in unto them. Therefore God dealt well with the midwives. Ex. 1: 18, 20.-- And there came forth a spirit, and stood before the Lord, and said, I will persuade him........, I will go forth and be a *lying spirit* in the mouth of all his prophets. And he said, Thou shalt persuade him and prevail also ; go forth and do so. 1 Kings 22: 21, 22.

Lying Forbidden.—Thou shalt *not* bear false witness. Ex. 20: 16. Lying lips are an abomination to the Lord. Prov. 12: 22. All *liars* shall have their part in the lake that burneth with fire and brim-stone. Rev. 21; 3.

In proposition 25 the great Author of all truth is accused of approving and sanctioning *lying*.— The case of Rahab is cited, and James 2 : 25 is quoted to prove that she was justified *for lying.* Truly this conclusion is " far-fetched " when the text says she was justified by *works,* because " she had received the messengers and sent them out another way." She was justified for what she *did* and not for what she *said.* The next case is that of the midwives, whom the king of Egypt commanded to destroy all the male children of the Hebrews. " But the midwives feared God and did not as the king of Egypt command-ed, but saved the male children alive.... *Therefore,* (because they feared God rather than man,) God dealt well with the midwives." Their defence before the king when reproved for their course, is another matter. God did not " deal well " with them as a reward for *what they told the king,* but for their *good works in saving the children alive.*

But how does the infidel know that what they told the king was false ? It still remains to be proven that they were guilty of falsehood at all.

Indeed it is more than likely in the light of History and Physiology that the midwives *told the truth* in respect to the hard-working daughters of Israel. For a reply to 1 Kings 22 : 21-22, see the harmony of Prop. 20.

26. *Hatred to the Edomite Sanctioned.*—He (Amaziah) slew of Edom, in the valley of Salt, ten thousand......... And he did that which was *right* in the sight of the Lord. 2 Kings 14: 7, 3.

Hatred to the Edomite Forbidden.—Thou shalt *not* abhor an Edomite, for he is thy *brother.* Deut. 22: 7.

Prop. 26 is certainly the most *bare-faced* and *dishonest* misrepresentation that we have ever seen. In this instance the infidel is obliged to quote the Bible backwards, skipping four verses at a time, in order to prove his position.

It is evident that he has a very difficult case on hand this time. He quotes 2 Kings 14 : 7, " He slew of Edom in the valley of salt ten thousand," and then skips backwards four verses, where the account of the king's reign begins, and quotes what was said of that monarch *while he was innocent of any man's blood* ; viz., that " He did that which was right in the sight of the Lord." Thus every principle of truth and honor—every sentiment of candor and fairness is sacrificed to prove that a God of justice has sanctioned crime. *We can use no language sufficiently strong, in condemning such palpable dishonesty.*

27. *Killing Commanded.*—Thus saith the Lord God of Israel, Put every man his sword by his side, and go in and out from gate to gate throughout the camp, and *slay* every man his brother, and every man his companion, and every man his neighbor. Ex. 32; 27.

Killing Forbidden.—Thou *shalt not kill.* Ex. 20: 13.

The skeptic here quotes Ex. 32: 27 to prove that God has commanded murder. This is a record of one of the severest judgments of Jehovah upon a people who had repeatedly trampled upon his laws and defied his power—they had sinned in the face of his mercy and rebelled in the midst of his fatherly care. Therefore, he pronounces upon their guilty heads the penalty of death. The tender hearted skeptic appears to be opposed to capital punishment. The laws of America forbid murder, but capital punishmhnt is still in force for the worst of crimes, and because it is thus inflicted, does it follow that the statutes of our country *contradict themselves*, and that they sanction murder, by hanging a criminal? The infidel's idea of justice (if indeed he has any,) appears to be strangely perverted.

28. *The Blood-shedder Must Die.*—At the hand of every man's brother will I require the *life* of man. Whoso sheddeth man's blood, by man shall his blood be shed. Gen. 9: 5. 6.

The Blood-shedder must Not Die.—And the Lord set a mark upon Cain, lest any finding him should *kill* him. Gen. 4: 15.

This is another specimen of "skipping backwards," in order to manufacture a contradiction. He quotes the law which pronounces the penalty upon murder in Gen. 9, and then goes back five chapters and quotes the 4th chapter to prove that God violated His own law, *sixteen hundred and fifty-five years before it was ever made! ! !* Such brazen efforts to garble the Bible must excite the pity of every candid reader.

29. *The Making of Images Forbidden.*—Thou shalt *not* make unto thee any graven image, or any likeness of anything that is in the heaven above, or that is in the earth beneath. Ex. 20: 4.

The Making of Images Commanded.—Thou shalt make two *cherubim* of gold......... And the cherubim shall stretch forth their wings on high, covering the mercy seat with their wings, and their faces shall look one to another. Ex. 25: 18, 20,

In Exodus 20: 4 men are forbidden to make

"unto themselves" any graven image—that is, they are commanded to *worship* nothing which is made by their own hands; and in Exodus 25, where we find the instructions relative to the building of the Ark of the Covenant it reads, "Thou shalt make two cherubims of gold," &c.— The first command forbids the *worship of images*, the second sanctions the creation of a beautiful symbol over the "mercy seat" of Jehovah. It was made "unto" God, and not "unto themselves." It was not the object of worship, but the beautiful type of a glorious future! Cannot the Deity forbid the worship of idols, and at the same time permit his people to erect the golden symbols of his love and mercy without contradicting Himself, and violating His own law?

30. *Slavery and Oppression Ordained.*—Cursed be Canaan: a *servant of servants* shall he be unto his brethren. Gen. 9: 25. Of the children of the strangers that do sojourn among you, of them shall ye buy......... They shall be your *bondmen forever;* but over your brethren of the children of Israel, ye shall not *rule with rigor.* Lev. 25: 45, 46. I will *sell* your sons and daughters into the hands of the children of Judah, and they shall *sell* them to the Sabeans, to a people afar off; for the *Lord* hath spoken it. Joel 3: 8.

Slavery and Oppression Forbidden.—Undo the heavy burdens......... Let the oppressed go free......... *break every yoke.* Isa. 58: 6. Thou shalt *neither* vex a stranger, nor *oppress* him. Ex. 22: 27,— He that *stealeth a man,* and *selleth him,* or if he be found in his hand, he shall surely be put to death. Ex. 21: 16. Neither be ye called *masters.* Matt. 23: 10.

We now come to the 30th problem of the *Infidels' Arithmetic,* for the work we are reviewing is the *text-book* of nearly every skeptic in the land. In this instance, God is charged with *ordaining slavery and oppression.* Gen. 9: 25 is simply a *prophecy* of what *would* come to pass in the future; it is *not* a decree of what *shall be.* Lev. 25: 45, 46 is so well explained by the following

note from Dr. Cheever, that we insert it entire.—
He says

"Let us now read along with this, the passage
in Lev. 25: 46, relating to the heathen servant or
servants coming from the heathen nations into
Judea for employment, and engaged under the
same jubilee-contract* the *forever contract,* as in
the preceding instance of the Hebrew servant so
engaged. It reads thus : 'Ye shall take them as
an inheritance for your children after you, to inherit a possession ; ye shall serve yourselves with
them forever.' As we have said, the phraseology
is almost *exactly the same* in the last clause, defin-
ing the extent of the contract with the heathen
servant, as in the clause in Exo. 21: 6, which defined the extent of the contract with the Hebrew
servant ; the word forever, being used in both
cases, and used with the same meaning, that is of
a contract extending till the jubilee. The word
bondman or bondmen, *is not used in either passage,* though our translators have chosen to put it
in the text, in the passage applying to the heathen,
but without the least authority or reason for so
doing. Instead of saying *they shall be your bondmen forever,* the passage simply says, just as concerning the Hebrew servant in Exodus, 'they
shall *serve* you forever ;' that is they shall be your
servants for the longest period admitted by your
laws for any service or contract, even till the *jubilee.* And as engaged by such contract, and paid
on such terms, ye do take them and may take
them, as an inheritance for your children after
you, *for any part of the term of service unexpired,*
when you the head of the family, are taken
away from your household. Then these servants

* According to the Bible laws, all servants were released
from their servitude at the end of each period of 50 years,
or *jubilee-periods,* for proof of which please read the whole
of the 25th chapter of Lev.

by you engaged and paid for an apprenticeship, till the jubilee, shall be for your children to inherit as a possession—the possession of their time and service, which by your contract with them, as rightfully belong to *your children* as to *you*, until the stipulated period comes to an end. *That* is the jubilee contract, the *forever-contract*. The passage in Ex. 21: 6, is absolute demonstration in regard to this matter.

" And thus are all the refuges of lies swept away, by which the advocates of slavery, (asserting that the heathen were slaves to the Hebrews, or could be held as such,) endeavor to make men believe that slavery is sanctioned by the law of God. See " God against Slavery," pages 156–7.

Joel 3: 8, is a *prophecy* of God's judgments upon the enemies of his people : " And they have cast lots for my people, and have given a boy for a harlot, and sold a girl for wine, that they might drink. Yea, and what have ye to do with me, O Tyre and Zidon, and all the coasts of Palestine, will ye render me a recompense, and if ye recompense me, swiftly and speedily will I return your recompense upon your own head ? Because ye have taken my silver, and my gold, and have carried into your temples my goodly pleasant things. The children also of Judah, and the children of Jerusalem, ye have sold unto the Grecians, that ye might remove them far from their border. Behold I will raise them out of the place whither ye have sold them, and will return your recompense upon your own head. And I will sell *your* sons and *your* daughters into the hand of the children of Judah, and they shall sell them to the Sabeans, to a people far off, for the Lord hath spoken it."

It was the recompense returned upon their own heads, *because* they had sold the children of Judah into bondage, they must undergo the *same* punishment they had put upon God's people. Every candid reader will acknowledge the justice of this penalty.

31. Improvidence Enjoined.—Consider the lillies of the field, how they grow; they toil not, neither do they spin......... If God so clothe the grass of the field.........shall he not much more cloth you ? .... Therefore, take no thought, saying, What shall we eat? or What shall we drink? or Wherewithal shall we be clothed ?......... Take no thought for the morrow. Matt. 6: 28, 31, 34. Give to every man that asketh of thee, and of him that taketh away thy goods, ask them not again......... And lend, hoping for nothing again, and your reward shall be great. Luke 6: 30, 35. Sell that ye have and give alms. Luke 12: 3.

Improvidence Condemned.—But if any provide not for his own, and especially for those of his own house, he hath denied the faith, and is worse than an infidel. 1 Tim. 5: 8. A good man leaveth an inheritance to his childrens' children. Prov. 13: 22.

The two texts which seem to oppose each other in the above, are Matt. 6: 31, 34, and 1 Tim. 5: 8. McKnight's translation from the original Greek, obviates the difficulty. "Therefore, say not anxiously.... what shall we eat, &c..... Be not then *anxious* about the morrow.... sufficient for the day is its own trouble." Matthew and Luke teach us to trust in Him who feedeth the ravens, while Timothy and Proverbs urge us not to become indolent, for we " must work while the day lasts." Surely there is no contradiction here.— While we are instructed to be industrious, and economical in the expenditure of our means, we are to avoid *anxiety*, in reference to the future supply of our wants, for if we seek *first* the Kingdom of God and His righteousness, all these things shall be added unto us.

32. Anger Approved.—Be ye angry and sin not. Eph. 4: 26.

Anger Disapproved.—Be not hasty in thy spirit to be angry: for anger resteth in the bosom of fools. Eccl. 7: 9. Make no friendship with an angry man. Prov. 22: 24. The wrath of man worketh not the righteousness of God. James 1: 20.

Ephesians 4: 26 is thus rendered by *Belsham.* "If ye be angry, yet sin not," and in this version he is sustained by Wakefield, Newcome, Bowyer, Beza, and Grotius.

The words, says Dr. Whitby, are not a command to be angry, but a caution to avoid *sinful* anger, hence all *apparent* discrepancy is obviated.

33. *Good Works to be Seen of Men.*—Let your light so shine before men, that they may see your good works. Matt. 5: 16.

Good Works Not to be Seen of Men.—Take heed that ye do not your alms before men, to be seen of them. Matt. 6: 1.

To the casual reader, these passages might appear inharmonious, especially as the skeptic has left out an *important* part of the first text. The *beauty* of the passage will be seen by quoting it entire. "Let your light so shine before men that they may see your good works, and *glorify* your Father which is in Heaven."

In Matt. 5: 16, we are taught to let the light of truth so shine, that men may be constrained to glorify God. Whereas, Matt. 6: 1, forbids the giving of alms, for the purpose of being *seen* of men, that we may receive the praises of the multitude. Truly,

"God is his own interpreter,
And He will make it plain."

The harmony of the text teaches us to work with reference to the glory of God, instead of our own glory.

34. *Judging of others Forbidden.*—Judge not, that ye be not judged. For with what judgment ye judge, ye shall be judged.— Matt. 7: 1, 2.

Judging of others Approved.—Do ye not know that the saints shall judge the world? And if the world shall be judged by you, are ye unworthy to judge the smallest matters? Know ye not that we shall judge angels? How much more things that pertain to this life? If, then, ye have judgments of things pertaining to this life, set them to judge who are least esteemed in the church. 1 Cor. 6: 2. 3, 4. Do not ye judge them that are within? 1 Cor. 5: 12.

The points of discrepancy which are made to appear in the above passages, are derived purely from wresting them from their context. The text in Matt. 7: 1, 2, has specific reference to a rash condemnatory spirit, which Jesus here highly reprehends, and warns his disciples against indulging in any course so-unjust and wrong.

1 Cor. 6: 2–4, refers to the period of the millennial reign of Christ when the saints will be joint rulers with him, executing the judgments of Jehovah upon the ungodly and the sinners against God's law, "and at which time they will be seated on thrones of judgment, and reigning on the earth as "Kings and Priests" with Christ. In proof of this, read in connection with 1 Cor. 6: 2, 4, Ps. 149: 5–9; Rev. 5: 9, 10; Matt. 19: 28; Rev. 20: 4–6; Dan. 7: 13, 14, 18, 21, 27. The last text quoted by the infidel, is 1 Cor. 5: 12.— A simple reading of the passage with its connections, will satisfy the reader that it has reference to excluding from christian fellowship., those who are unworthy the name of Christ. In the light of these facts we would ask the candid reader where the skeptic has any ground for offering these passages, as opposed to each other. But we have had, and probably shall continue to have, occasion to expose many cases equally palpable and unjust.

35. Christ taught Non-resistance.—Resist not evil, but whosoever shall smite thee on thy right cheek, turn to him the other also. Matt. 5: 39. All they that take the sword shall perish with the sword. Matt. 26: 52.

Christ Taught and Practised Physical Resistance.—He that hath no sword, let him sell his garment and buy one. Luke 22: 36.— And when he had made a scourge of small cords, he drove them all out of the temple. John 2; 15.

Agreeable to Matt. 5: 39, we are taught not to avenge ourselves or *resist evil*. The promotion of the christian religion does not depend upon carnal weapons nor the sword. The skeptic however, would have it appear that because Christ instructed his disciples just before he was taken and crucified, to sell their garments and buy swords, &c., that he taught physical resistance.— Whereas, the truth is, that when informed that there were *two* swords, he said they were enough. But they were *not* enough if they were to have a combat and resist those sent to take him, but they were enough for the purpose for which Jesus wished them, and that was to *practically* illustrate his *mercy* and *kindness*, for when Peter cut off the servant's ear, Jesus rebuked him for his rash act, and healed the bleeding wound. Hence from this circumstance we learn that Christ was a practical example of his own teaching. We conceive the foregoing to be all that it is necesary to notice.

36. *Christ Warned his followers not to fear being killed.* Be not *afraid* of them that *kill* the body. Luke 11: 4.

Christ himself avoided the Jews for fear of being killed.— After these things Jesus walked in Galilee; for he would not walk in Jewry, because the Jews sought to *kill* him. John 7: 1.

Luke 12: 4, (not 11: 4, as above quoted,) is simply an exhortation to fear God rather than man. It teaches that we are not to shape our conduct to please the world, but to obey the commands of God, fearless of man's opposition, for "I, even I, am he that comforteth you, who art thou that thou shouldst be afraid of a *man* that shall die, and of the son of man which shall be made as grass, and *forgettest* the] Lord thy Maker that hath stretched forth the heavens and laid the foundations of the earth."

John 7: 1, is an evidence simply that Christ sought to preserve his own life until the *time* came for him to be offered up. Did he not give up his life *cheerfully*, when the hour was come? He was a *willing* sacrifice for our sins. His blood was spilled even for those who are spending time in villifying His pure character, and charging the Son of God with falsehood. We may search in vain amid the records of the dark ages for ingratitude so base and black as *this*, which thus blots the pages of modern civilization.

37. *Public Prayer Sanctioned.*—And Solomon stood before the altar of the Lord in the presence of all the congregation of Israel, and spread forth his hand toward heaven. (Then follows the prayer.) And it was so, that when Solomon had made an end of praying all this prayer and supplication unto the Lord, he arose from before the altar of the Lord, from kneeling on his knees, with his hands spread up to heaven......... And the Lord said unto him, I have heard thy prayer and thy supplication that thou hast made before me.— 1 Kings 8: 22, 54, and 1 Kings 9: 3.

Public Prayer Disapproved.—When thou prayest thou shalt not be as the hypocrites are: for they love to pray standing in the synagogues, and in the corners of the streets, that they may be seen of men......... But thou, when thou prayest, enter into thy closet, and when thou hast shut thy door, pray to thy Father which is in secret, Matt. 6: 5, 6.

The only text that seems to require any explanation in the above, is Matt. 6: 5, 6, and this is simply a record of the conduct of that class which is still represented in the 19th century, by those who make long and flowery speeches upon their knees, that they may be admired of men, and in opposition to this course, the disciples are admonished to secret prayer.

God's children are not forbidden to pray before men. Jesus, our great exampler, prayed before the multitude at the grave of Lázarus, and his followers may also thus acknowledge God before men, but we are forbidden to pray for the *purpose* of being seen of men, as well as to make long prayers for a *pretence*. Our instructions then by both precept and example, are, not to be ashamed of God or afraid to acknowledge before men our dependence upon Him. And as our great High Priest prayed before the multitude, we who try to follow his footsteps may do likewise. But we are also to remember that the most frequently sought solitude wherein to converse with the Most High, so also the great burden of the christian's prayer is in *secret*—in the closet or in the chamber, where God alone can hear and approve, and we have the promise of an *open reward*. Prayer is our only means of communion with the Most High. He has communicated with us by his word, but we only commune with him through the means which he himself has ordained for our benefit. And surely we cannot neglect this, our greatest *earthly* privilege.

**38. *Importuning in prayer Commended.*—Because this widow troubleth me, I will avenge her, lest by her continual coming she weary me......., And shall not God avenge his own elect, which cry day and night unto him? Luke 18: 5, 7. Because of his importunity he will rise and give him as many as he needeth. Luke 11: 8.

Importunity in prayer Condemned.—But when ye pray, use not vain repetitions as the heathen do; for they think that they shall be heard for their much speaking. Be ye not therefore like unto them ; for your Father knoweth what things ye have need of before ye ask him. Matt. 6: 7, 8.

· This proposition is so similar that it scarcely needs a reply. *Earnestness* and *constancy* of prayer are commended, while we are admonished not to use "vain repetitions, as the heathen do." The wise man says, be not rash with thy mouth, and let not thine heart be hasty to utter *any* thing before God, for God is in Heaven and thou upon earth, therefore let thy words be few." Hence, we are to approach the Majesty of the skies with becoming reverence; we are to avoid the customs which the heathen adopt in addressing their gods; for an illustration of which please see the worship of Baal, as recorded in 1 Kings 18: 26–29.

39. *The wearing of Long Hair by men Sanctioned.*—And *no razor* shall come on his head ; for the child shall be a Nazarite unto God from the womb. Judg. 13: 5. All the days of the vow of his separation there shall *no razor* come upon his head ; until the days be fulfilled in which he separateth himself unto the Lord, he shall be holy, and shall let the locks of the hair of his head grow. Num. 6: 5.

The wearing of Long Hair by men Condemned.—Doth not even nature itself teach you, that if a man have *long hair*, it is a *shame* unto him? 1 Cor. 11: 14.

This only needs a simple remark to obviate all difficulty. We will state for the information (?) of the skeptic, that many customs and practices, which were sanctioned by the old Mosaic law, passed away and were rendered obsolete by the termination of that dispensation. Hence his quotation from the New Testament of a declaration which was made long after the fulfillment of the law, bears no evidence against the customs of the previous dispensation.

40. *Circumcision Instituted.*—This is my covenant which ye shall keep between me and you and thy seed after thee : Every man child among you shall be circumcised. Gen. 17: 10.

Circumcision Condemned.—Behold, I Paul, say unto you, that if ye be circumcised, Christ shall profit you nothing. Gal. 5: 2.

The infidel has made precisely the same mistake here that he made in the previous proposition. Circumscision was instituted in the days of Abraham, and incorporated into the Mosaic law, which was nailed to the cross, for " Christ is the end of the law." So Paul *was right* when he said, " that if ye be circumcised, Christ shall profit you nothing;" for to conform to the requirements of a law which he had rendered obsolete, was virtually, the rejection of him as the Messiah.

41. The Sabbath Instituted.—Remember the Sabbath day to keep it holy. Ex. 20: 8.

The Sabbath Repudiated.—The new moons and *sabbaths*, the calling of assemblies, I cannot away with ; it is iniquity. Isa. 1: 13. One man esteemeth one day above another: another esteemeth every day alike. Let every man be fully persuaded in his own mind,—Rom. 14: 5. Let no man therefore judge you in meat or drink, or in respect of a holy day, or of the new moon; or of the sabbath days. Gal. 4: 5.

The keeping of the seventh day, as holy time, was also instituted under the law and sanctioned by Jehovah in the Jewish dispensation. Isa. 1: 13 is addressed to a class of persons who had sinned so fearfully before the Lord, that their sacrifices were vain oblations, and their incense was an abomination unto Him. Therefore, He saith, " Bring no more vain oblations—incense is an abomination unto me—the new moons and Sabbaths—the calling of assemblies—I cannot away with—it is iniquity, *even* the solemn meeting.— Your new moons and your appointed feasts my soul hateth." They had sinned until even their worship was offensive to Deity, for " The prayers of the *wicked* are an *abomination* to the Lord."— Hence He says, " When ye spread forth your hands, I will hide mine eyes from you ; yea, when ye make many prayers, I will not hear.— *Your hands are full of blood.*" Does not *this* sufficiently explain why their new moons and Sabbaths were distasteful to God? But the keeping of the seventh day passed away with the law of which it was a component part. It is well to devote one day in the seven exclusively to the worship of God. The disciples met on the *first day* of the week, and it was also hallowed by the resurrection of our Lord. Hence we recognize THIS as the day of worship, but there is *now* no *law* of God which commands us to observe the Mosaic Sabbath. Hence Rom. 14: 5, and Gal. 4: 5 are to the point.

42. *The Sabbath instituted because God rested on the Seventh day.*—For in six days the Lord made heaven and earth, the sea, and all that in them is, and rested on the seventh day ; wherefore the Lord blessed the Sabbath day and hallowed it. Ex. 20: 11.

The Sabbath instituted beacause God brought the Israelites out of Egypt.—And remember that thou wast a servant in the land of Egypt, and that the Lord thy God brought thee out thence through a mighty hand and a stretched out arm : therefore the Lord thy God commanded thee to keep the Sabbath day. Deut. 5: 15.

Any close observer will see at once that there is no want of harmony here. Ex. 20 : 11 shows *why* "the Lord *blessed* the seventh day and *hallowed* it," and Deut. 5 : 15 shows why He commanded Israel to keep the Sabbath day, *after it was instituted.* So there is not even the semblance of a contradiction here. Comment is unnecessary.

43. *No Work to be done on the Sabbath under penalty of death,*—Whosoever doeth *any work* on the Sabbath day, he shall surely be put to death. Ex. 31: 15. And they found a man that gathered sticks upon the Sabbath day......... And all the congregation brought him without the camp and *stoned* him with stones, and he died: as the Lord commanded Moses. Num. 15: 32, 36.

Jesus Christ Broke the Sabbath and justified his Disciples in the same.—Therefore did the Jews persecute Jesus, and sought to slay him, because he had done these things on the Sabbath day John 5: 16. At that time Jesus went on the Sabbath day through the corn : and his disciples were a hungered, and began to pluck the ears of corn, and to eat. But when the Pharisees saw it they said unto him, Behold, thy disciples do that which is *not lawful* to do upon the Sabbath day. But he said unto them......... Have ye not read in the law, how that on the Sabbath days the priests in the temple profane the Sabbath, and are blameless? Matt. 12: 1, 2, 3, 5,

The Son of God is here accused of violating the Sabbath, and we answer the charge in the words of Jesus himself, "The Sabbath was made for man, and not the man for the Sabbath. *Therefore the Son of Man is Lord also of the Sabbath.*"

44. Baptism Commanded.—Go ye therefore and teach all nations, baptizing them in the name of the Father, and of the Son, and of the Holy Ghost. Matt. 28: 19.

Baptism Not Commanded.—For Christ sent me *not* to baptize, but to preach the gospel......... I thank God that I baptized none of you but Crispus and Gaius. 1 Cor. 1: 17, 14.

The infidel here quotes the commission for baptism and then takes advantage of the words of Paul and tries thereby to nulify the commission. This logic is so weak that it does not deserve any answer. Suppose Paul did not receive an *especial* commission to baptize, does that prove that Jesus gave no such commission to *any one?*— Shame upon such pitiful objections to God's word!

45. Every kind of Animal allowed for food.—Every moving thing that liveth shall be meat for you. Gen. 9: 3. Whatsoever is sold in the shambles that eat. 1 Cor. 10: 25. There is nothing unclean of itself. Rom. 14: 4.

Certain kinds of Animals Prohibited for food.—Nevertheless, these shall ye *not eat,* of them that chew the cud, or of them that divide the cloven hoof; as the camel and the hare, and the coney: for they chew the cud, but divide not the hoof: therefore, they are *unclean* unto you. And the *swine,* because it divideth the hoof, yet cheweth not the cud, it is unclean unto you; ye shall *not eat* of their flesh, nor touch their dead carcass. Deut. 14: 7, 8.

This is one of those propositions that needs no reply, but the fact that they belong to the series, crowds them upon our notice, so we will simply remark that Gen. 9 : 3 refers to a period eight hundred and ninety-seven years (according to the best chronology we have) before that law against the use of certain meats was enacted.

Deut. 14: 7-8 is a record of the enactment of that law. And 1 Cor. 10: 25, and Rom. 14: 14 were written, the one twenty-nine, and the other thirty years *after* the law was *abolished.* We think this explanation must prove satisfactory, even to an infidel.

46. *The taking of Oaths Sanctioned.*—If a man vow a vow unto the Lord, or swear an *oath* to bind his soul with a bond, he shall not break his word : he shall do according to all that proceedeth out of his mouth. Num. 30: 2. Now, therefore, *swear* unto me by God......... And Abraham said, I - will *swear*......... Therefore, he called the place Beersheba, (the well of the oath;) because there they sware both of them. Gen. 21: 23, 23, 25, 31. And Jacob *sware* by the fear of his father Isaac. Gen. 21: 35. Because he (God) could swear by no greater, he *sware* by himself. Heb. 6: 13.

The Taking of Oaths Forbidden.—But I say unto you, *swear not at all*, neither by heaven for it is God's throne; neither by the earth for it is his footstool. Matt. 5: 14.

Oaths were allowed under the old dispensation, and forbidden under the new. Had the skeptic been *aware* of the fact that *Christ was the end of the law* and *honest* enough to acknowledge it, it would have saved us much useless labor.

47. *Marriage Approved.*—And the Lord God said, it is not good that the man should be alone: I will make a help-meet for him.— Gen. 2: 18. And God said unto them, Be fruitful and multiply and replenish the earth. Gen. 1; 28. For this cause shall a man leave father and mother and shall cleave unto his wife. Matt. 19: 5. Marriage is honorable in all. Heb. 13: 4.

Marriage Disapproved.—It is good for man not to touch a woman. 1 Cor. 7: 1. For I (Paul) would that all men were 'even as I myself......... It is good for them if they abide even as I. 1 Cor, 7: 7, 8.

The compiler of the work before us here quotes Paul to nulify the marriage covenant, but he has, as usual, misrepresented the text and vilified its author. 1 Cor. 7: 1 so far from disapproving of marriage is actually addressed to *married people,* as the whole connection shows.—The 7th and 8th verses are addressed to *widows* and *widowers,* "I say therefore, to the *unmarried* and *widows,* it is good for them if they abide even as I." The word "unmarried" in the above text is *agamoi* and applies to those who have lost their companions, "It is good for them if they abide even as I." That is, it was good for them to remain in a widowed state, for according to the best historical evidence we can get, Paul was at this time a widower. The prevalent idea that Paul was a bachelor has no foundation, either in his epistles or in history. *Eusebius, Clement* and other authentic historians speak of him as a married man.

48. *Freedom of Divorce Permitted.*—When a man hath taken a wife and married her, and it came to pass that she found no favor in his eyes,.........then let him write her a bill of divorcement, and give it in her hand, and send her out of his house. Deut. 24: 1.— When thou goest out to war against thine enemies, and the Lord thy God hath delivered them into thy hands, and thou hast taken them captive, and seeest among the captives a beautiful woman and hast a desire unto her, then thou shalt take her home to thy house;......... and after that thou shalt go in unto her and be her husband, and she shall be thy wife.......... And if thou have no delight in her, then thou shalt let her go whither she will; but thou shalt not sell her at all for money; thou shalt not make merchandize of her. Deut. 21: 10, 11, 14.

***Divorce Restricted.*—**But I say unto you, that whosoever shall put away his wife, saving for the cause of fornication, causeth her to commit adultery. Matt. 5: 32.

The reader will see at once that the texts quoted in Deuteronomy, refer to the Mosaic Dispensation, and that in Matthew is the law of Christ. Our *learned historian* (?) has made this *blunder* so often, that we are weary of correcting him. Had he omitted that class of contradictions, "falsely so called," his propositions would have been few indeed.

49. *Adultery Forbidden.*—Thou shalt not commit adultery.— Ex. 20: 14. Whoremongers and adulterers, God will judge.—Heb. 13: 4.

Adultery Allowed.—But all the women children that have not known a man by lying with him, keep alive for yourselves. Num.— 31: 18. And the Lord said unto Hosea, Go, take thee a wife of whoredoms.........Then said the Lord to me [Hosea,] Go yet, love a woman, beloved of her friend, yet an adultress. So I bought her; and said unto her, Thou shalt abide for me many days; thou shalt not play the harlot, and thou shalt not be for another man; so will I also be to thee.—Hos. 1: 2; Hos. 2: 1, 2, 3

Num. 31: 18, is here quoted to prove that Moses authorized the Israelites to make concubines of the whole number of female children. But the whole tenor of the law, and especially the statute recorded in Deut. 21: 10–14, proves most decisively to the contrary. They were merely permitted to possess them as female slaves, educating them in their families, and employing them as domestics—for the laws concerning fornication, concubinage and marriage, forbade an Israelite from even *marrying* a captive, without delays and previous formalities. If the reader will study the whole connection of Hosea 1: he will see that under the figure of a wife proving false to her marriage vows, and bearing children likely to follow her example, the prophet represents the shameful idolatry of Israel which provoked God to cast them off. The whole passage conveys information by action, instead of words. That is, it is an allegorical representation of the ingratitude and unfaithfulness of the nation. The Lord had provided for and protected Israel. He had cared for them as a thoughtful husband cares for his wife, and they owed the fidelity of a wife to a tender

3

husband. Instead of this, however, they had long addicted themselves to *spiritual* fornication or idolatry. (See Cottage Bible.)

50. Marriage or Cohabitation with a Sister Denounced.— Cursed is he that lieth with his *sister*, the daughter of his father.— Deut. 27: 22. And if a man shall take a *sister*, his father's daughter, or his mother's daughter,.........it is a wicked thing.—Lev. 20: 17.

Abraham Married his Sister and God Blessed the Union.— And Abraham said,......... She is my *sister*; she is the daughter of my father, but not the daughter of my mother.—Gen. 20: 11, 12. And God said unto Abraham, as for Sarah thy wife,......... I will bless her, and give thee a son also of her.—Gen. 17: 16.

The Bible indeed denounces marriage with a sister, but the truthful declaration of Abraham was made *four hundred and seven years* before any law was enacted against the marriage of near relatives Says Dr. Sleigh, "There are two very obvious reasons why at the *beginning*, near relations were not prohibited intermarrying.

1. No physical evil arises from it till repeated through several generations.

2. In the beginning, as it seemed fit to the Creator that the earth should be populated from one pair, it was indispensably necessary for even brothers and sisters to marry, but as generations began to increase, the necessity became diminished, and the physical evil increased, till it seemed good to the Almighty to give specific directions on the subject..... Since that time, of course, intermarriage with near relations, has been criminal."

51. A man may Marry his Brother's Widow.—If brethren dwell together, and one of them die and have no child, the wife of the dead shall not marry without unto a stranger; her husband's brother shall come in unto her and take her to wife.—Deut. 25: 5.

A man may Not Marry his Brother's Widow.—If a man shall take his brother's wife, it is an unclean thing..,......., they shall be childless.—Lev. 20: 21,

Lev. 20: 21 forbids a man taking his brother's WIFE, while Deut. 25: 5 permits him to marry his brother's WIDOW. The difference is obvious.— While a woman's husband *lives*, she is a *wife*, but at his *death* she ceases to be a *wife* and becomes a *widow*. Hence Lev. 20: 21 is simply an enactment against adultery.

52. Hatred to Kindred Enjoined.—If any man come unto me, and hate not his father, and mother, and wife, and children, and brother, and sisters, yea, and his own life also, he cannot be my disciple.—Luke 14: 26.

Hatred to Kindred Condemned.—Honor thy father and mother. —Eph: 6: 2. Husbands love your wives.......... For no man ever ye hateth his own flesh.—Eph. 5: 25, 29. Whosoever hateth his brother is a murderer.—1 John 3: 15.

In Luke 14: 26 the word *hate* merely signifies to *love less*. Please notice that a man is commanded to hate *his own life* in the same sense that he is commanded to hate his relatives. The meaning of the text evidently is, that he who so loves his father and mother or *his own flesh* as to obey any of their impulses, orders or directions, in opposition to the commands of God, " *cannot be my disciple.*" It is evident that according to Scripture usage, the word *hate* simply means to love less—thus in Proverbs we find the declaration, "He that spareth the rod hateth his son."— If our affections are placed upon God and His Son, everything else will be of minor importance.

53. Intoxicating Beverages Recommended.—Give *strong drink* to him that is ready to perish, and *wine* to those that be of heavy hearts. Let him drink and forget his poverty, and remember his misery no more.—Prov. 31: 6, 7. Drink no longer water, but use a little *wine* for thy stomach's sake, and thine often infirmities.—1 Tim 5: 23. *Wine maketh glad* the heart of man.—Ps. 104: 15.

Intoxicating Beverages Discountenanced.—Wine is a mocker. strong drink is raging, and whosoever is deceived thereby, is not wise, —Prov. 20: 1. Look not upon the wine when it is red; when it giveth his color in the cup........., At the last it biteth like a serpent and stingeth like an adder.—Prov. 23: 31, 32,

The first three texts simply recommend the use of wine for medicinal purposes, and the last two forbid its use as a *beverage*. Such foolish objections are a *shame* to the boasted intellect of manhood.

54. *It is our Duty to obey Rulers, who are God's Ministers and punish Evil Doers only.*—Let every soul be subject unto the higher powers. For there is no power but of God; the powers that be are ordained of God. Whosoever, therefore, resisteth the power, resisted the ordinance of God; and they that resist shall receive to themselves damnation. For rulers are not a terror to good works, but to evil......... For this cause pay ye tribute: for they are God's ministers, attending continually upon this very thing,—Rom. 13: 1, 2, 3, 6. The Scribes and Pharisees sit in Moses' seat; all, therefore, whatsoever they bid you observe, that observe and do.—Matt. 23: 2, 3. *Submit* yourselves to every ordinance of man for the Lord's sake ; whether it be to the king as supreme, or unto governors as unto them that are sent of him for the punishment of evil doers.—1 Pet. 2: 13, 14. I counsel thee to keep the king's commandment .... Whoso keepeth the commandment shall feel no evil thing.—Eccl. 8: 2, 5.

It is Not our Duty always to obey Rulers, who Sometimes punish the good, and receive unto themselves Damnation therefor.—But the midwives feared God, and did not as the king of Egypt command them ..... Therefore God dealt well with the midwives.—Ex. 1: 17. 20. Shadrach, Meshach, and Abednego answered and said......... Be it known unto thee, O king, that we will not serve thy gods, nor worship the golden image which thou hast set up.— Dan. 3: 16, 18. Therefore, king Darius signed the writing and the decree......... (that whosoever shall ask a petition of any God for thirty days.........he shall be cast into the den of lions) .... Now, when Daniel knew that the writing was signed, he went into his house and ....kneeled upon his knees three times a day and prayed.........as he did aforetime.—Dan. 6: 9, 7, 10. And the rulers were gathered together against the Lord and against his Christ. For of a truth, against thy holy child Jesus, whom thou hast anointed, both Herod and Pontius Pilate, with the Gentiles, and the people of Israel, were gathered together.—Acts 4: 26, 27. Beware of the Scribes, which love to go in long clothing, and love salutations in the market places, and the chief seats in the synagogues........., These shall receive greater *damnation.*—Mark 12: 38, 39, 40. And Herod with his men of war set him at naught, and mocked him, and arrayed him in a gorgeous robe, and sent him again to Pilate......... And Pilate gave sentence......... and when they were come to the place which is called Calvary, there they crucified him......... And the people stood by beholding. And the rulers also with them derided him.—Luke 23: 11, 24, 33, 35,

The long array of texts here quoted, simply teaches God's children to obey every law of the " powers that be," that is founded in justice and equity. When any State law conflicts with the National constitution, it is not our duty to obey it, so when human law conflcts with the law of God, we are not to bow to the lesser, but yield our obedience to the great Law-giver of the Universe.— " Render to Cesar the things that are Cesar's, and to God the things that are God's." Hence, whenever we can obey rulers and magistrates without conflicting with the law of God, we are Scripturally bound to do so. But if men legislate against God and His truth, our obligation to them ceases; for instance, the Fugitive Slave law was made by man, but it conflicted with God's command to do to others as we would that they should do to us, hence no christian could consistently act up to its requirements. The immortal Blackstone—England's pre-eminent jurist—well remarks that " An *enactment* is *not* a *law*, when it conflicts with the law of God."

55. *Woman's Rights Denied.*—And thy desire shall be to thy husband, and he shall *rule* over thee.—Gen. 3: 16. I suffer not a woman to teach, nor usurp authority over a man, but to be in *silence.*— 1 Tim. 2: 12. They are commanded to be under *obedience*, as also saith the law.—1 Cor. 14: 34, Even as Sarah *obeyed* Abraham, calling him Lord.—1 Pet. 3: 6,

***Woman's Rights Affirmed.*—**And Deborah, a prophetess,... *judged* Israel at that time......... And Deborah said unto Barak, Up. for this is the day in which the Lord hath delivered Sisera into thy hand........., And the Lord discomfited Sisera, and all his chariots, and all his host, with the edge of the sword before Barak.—Judges 4: 4, 14, 15. The inhabitants of the villages ceased; they ceased in Israel, until I, Deborah, arose, a mother in Israel.—Judg. 5: 7. And on my hand-maidens I will pour out in those days my spirit, and they shall prophesy.—Acts 2: 18. And the same man had four daughters, virgins, which did prophesy.—Acts 21: 9.

Because a woman is taught to render due respect to her husband and not to usurp authority over him; because women were forbidden to habitually speak in public, or to interfere with matters which it was a man's business to attend to—does it therefore follow that when the Lord pours out his spirit upon them, that they are still to be silent? If God bestows an extraordinary gift upon a woman, or gives her a work to do, no apostle of Jesus would forbid her. Anna was allowed to prophesy in the temple as well as Simeon. And Paul's prohibition of a woman's praying or prophesying *unveiled* was certainly an acknowledgment of her right to do so, under such a regulation. Hence the Bible gives to woman a position of dignity, and also of delicacy —it points out the true sphere in which she is to act with becoming modesty and self-respect.

56. Obedience to Masters Enjoined.—Servants *obey* in all things your masters after the flesh. And whatsoever ye do, do it as heartily as to the Lord.—Col. 3: 22, 23. Be *subject* to your *masters* with all fear; not only to the good and gentle, but also to the froward.—1 Pet. 2: 18.

Obedience Due to God Only.—Thou shalt worship the Lord thy God, and him only shalt thou *serve.*—Matt. 4: 10. Be *not* ye the servants of men.—1 Cor. 7: 23. Neither be ye called masters: for one is your master, even Christ.—Matt. 23: 10.

The passages in the first part of this proposition simply teach servants to obey their masters in matters relating to their regular employment. But the infidel thinks he finds a contradiction of this in Matt. 4: 10, which teaches that the "Lord thy God" is the only object of worship, but it requires little discernment to see that this passage has no reference to secular things. He also quotes 1 Cor. 7: 23, which reads, "Ye are bought with a price; be not ye the servants of men."— Christ having given his life for the saints, they are to obey Him in preference to men. There is surely no contradiction here for the texts quoted in the first part of the proposition, no where teach that servants are to obey their masters in preference to Christ.

Matt. 23: 10 is an admonition to the saints, which forbids the assumption of titles.

57. *There is an Unpardonable Sin.*—He that shall blaspheme against the Holy Ghost hath never forgiveness.—Mark 3: 29.

***There is No Unpardonable Sin.*—**And by him all that believe are justified from all things.—Acts 13: 39.

The key to this problem is found in the latter part of the text last quoted, and which the infidel was obliged to leave off in order to make out his "contradiction." The text reads thus:— "And by him all that believe are justified from all things from which ye could not be justified *by the law of Moses.*" By quoting the whole text, the difficulty is at once obviated. There was no justification in the law of Moses, as will appear from Rom. 3: 20; "Therefore by the deeds of the law, there shall no flesh be justified in His sight; for by the law is the knowledge of sin." It is not the province of law to justify, but to condemn those who transgress. Hence, in the New Testament, justification is attributed to the grace of Jesus Christ. The unpardonable sin mentioned in Mark could not be committed under the dispensation of the law. Hence, Acts 13: 39 has no reference to it whatever. The unpardonable sin consists in an apostacy from the truth of the gospel. "For it is impossible for those who were once enlightened and have tasted of the heavenly gift and were made partakers of the Holy Ghost, and have tasted the good word of God and the powers of the world to come, if they shall fall away to renew them again unto repentance, seeing they crucify to themselves the Son of God afresh, and put him to an open shame."—Heb. 6: 4, 6.

58. Man was Created After the other Animals.—And God made the beasts of the earth after his kind, and the cattle after their kind......... And God said, Let us make *man*.. So God created man in his own image.—Gen. 1: 25, 26.

Man was Created Before the other Animals.—And the Lord God said it is not good that *man* should be *alone*: I will make a help-meet for him. And out of the ground the Lord God formed every *beast* of the field, and every fowl of the air, and brought them unto Adam to see what he would call them.—Gen. 2: 18, 19.

The latter part of Gen. 2: 18, 19, is simply a repetition of Gen. 1: 25-26. The idea from the original Hebrew would perhaps be more clearly expressed by the following rendering: "The Lord God brought every beast of the field and every fowl of the air (which he had formed out of the ground,) unto Adam to see what he would call them." The mere redundancy of expression is a frivolous pretext for a cavil.

59. Seed time and Harvest were Never to Cease.—While the earth remaineth, seed time and harvest.........shall not cease.—Gen 8: 22.

Seed time and Harvest Did Cease for Seven Years.—And the seven years of *dearth* began to come......... And the *famine* was over all the face of the earth.—Gen. 41: 54, 56. For these two years hath *famine* been in the land; and yet there are five years in which there shall *neither be earing nor harvest.*—Gen. 45: 6.

This "contradiction" (like many others,) has been manufactured by wresting a text from its connection. Gen. 8: 22 is simply a promise of the change of seasons. The true elipsis of the text is as follows: "Seed time and harvest time shall not cease." God has no where promised us a crop of grain every year, but simply

that seed time and harvest time shall continue.—
This is evident not only from the grammatical
construction of language, but from the whole
connection. The verse reads as follows:—
" While the earth remaineth, seed time and
harvest (time) and cold and heat and ·summer
and winter and day and night shall not cease "

60. *God Hardened Pharaoh's Heart.*—But I will *harden* his
heart, that he shall not let the people go.—Ex. 4: 21. And the Lord
hardened the *heart* of Pharaoh.—Ex. 9: 12.

Pharaoh Hardened his Own Heart.—But when Pharaoh saw
that there was respite, *he hardened his heart,* and hearkened not
unto them.—Ex. 8: 15.

This proposition admits of the most easy solution. Both texts are strictly true. God was the
cause of hardening Pharaoh's heart, because he
it was who offered mercies to the wicked king,
upon conditions of obedience : and on the other
hand it is equally true that Pharaoh hardened his
own heart, because he resisted the kindness and
mercy of God, and brought desolation and ruin
upon himself and kingdom

61. *All the Cattle and Horses in Egypt Died.*—Behold, the
hand of the Lord is upon thy cattle which is in the field, upon the
horses, upon the asses, upon the camels, upon the oxen, and upon
the sheep......... And *all the cattle of Egypt died.*—Ex. 9: 3, 6.

All the Horses of Egypt did Not Die.—But the Egyptians pursued after them (all the *horses* and chariots of Pharaoh, and his
horsemen, and his army) and overtook them encamping by the sea.
Ex. 14: 9.

The infidel here endeavors to prove first, that
all the horses of Egypt were slain by God's
judgment ; and second, that they pursued the
children of Israel with horses. But it is very
evident that their horses were not all killed (if indeed any of them were,) from the following facts :

1st. The threat simply includes the animals in the field, and the horses belonging to the royal service could not have been laboring in the field; and there were probably many others also that were not there.

2d. The record only says that "all the *cattle* of Egypt died." It does not say that the horses died also. And it will be noticed that the disease which was sent upon the cattle to destroy them, was the *murrain*—a disease not likely to attack horses!

3d. The words, both in the Hebrew and Greek, which are rendered "all" in our version in many instances, simply mean "many," or a "large proportion of," "a majority." For instance; "*All* Judea went out to be baptised of John in Jordan;" still we have accounts of a certain class that did not go. See also the declaration that "death has passed upon all men," yet we have the history of two men who never died. Hence we may safely infer that the term is used in the same legitimate sense in the text before us.

**62. *Moses Feared Pharaoh.*—And Moses *feared*, and said, Surely this thing is known. Now, when Pharaoh heard this thing, he sought to slay Moses. But Moses fled before the face of Pharaoh, and dwelt in the land of Midian......... And it came to pass, in process of time, that the king of Egypt died. And the Lord said unto Moses, in Midian, Go, return unto Egypt; for all the men are dead that sought thy life. Ex. 2: 14, 15 ; Ex. 23. Ex. 4: 19.

Moses Did Not Fear Pharaoh.—By faith he [Moses] forsook Egypt, *not fearing* the wrath of the king.—Heb. 11: 27.**

The texts quoted in Exodus refer to Moses' flight from Egypt at the time he slew the Egyptian, at which time it is very evident that he feared the wrath of Pharoah. But Heb. 11: 27 refers explicitly to the time when Moses left Egypt with the children of Israel, and as at this time he was acting directly in harmony with the express commands of Jehovah, he had no cause to fear an earthly tyrant.

63. There Died of the Plague Twenty-four Thousand.—And those that died in the plague were twenty and four thousand.—Num. 25: 9.

There Died of the Plague but Twenty-three Thousand.—And fell in one day three and twenty thousand.—1 Cor. 10: 8.

This problem in clearly explained by Bagster's note upon the first text which we insert " St. Paul reckons only 23,000, though some manuscripts and versions, particularly the latter, Syrian and Armenian have as here 24,000; allowing the 24,000 to be genuine, (and none of the Hebrew manuscripts exhibit a various reading here,) and the 23,000 of St. Paul to be also genuine, the two places may be reconciled by supposing, what is very probable that Moses includes in the 24,000 the 1,000 men who were slain, in consequence of the judicial examination, (verse 4,) as well as the 23,000 who died of the plague, while St. Paul only refers to the latter. Hence it is clear that the whole number of those who died of the plague was 24,000, while it is equally true, as Paul says, that " there fell, *in one day*, three and twenty thousand."

64. John the Baptist was Elias.—This is Elias which was to come.—Matt. 11: 14.

John the Baptist was Not Elias.—And they asked him, What then? Art thou Elias? and he said I am not.—John 1: 21.

Matt. 11: 14 reads, " If ye will receive it, this is Elias which was for to come."

The reader will see at once by the pronoun used in the foregoing text, that it does not refer to the *person* of Elias. It simply conveys the idea that John the Baptist was the forerunner, or the Elias of the *first* advent, as Elias *himself* is to be the forerunner of the *second*. If we should say that Abraham Lincoln was the Washington of the 19th century, no one would suppose that we intended to convey the idea that he was *in fact* George Washington. And although John was indeed the *Elias*, or forerunner of the first advent of the Messiah, yet in reply to the question "Art thou Elias," (*i. e.* the veritable prophet,) he truthfully answers, *I am not.* His position is easily explained by the text, which says, "He came in the spirit and power of Elias."

65. *The Father of Joseph, Mary's Husband, was Jacob.*— And Jacob begat Joseph, the husband of Mary, of whom was born Jesus.—Matt. 1: 16.

The Father of Mary's Husband was Heli.—Being the son of Joseph which was the son of Heli.—Luke 3: 23.

This problem is easily solved by the following considerations: It is evident, from Matt. 1: 16, that Jacob was the *natural* father of Joseph, while Heli was the father of Mary, his wife; and as Mary was the only child and heiress of Heli (according to the Talmud) when Joseph married her, he became the only son and heir of Heli.— The Jews often traced genealogy in this way, "For instance, in 1 Chron. 2: 22, Jair is reckoned among the posterity of Judah: because the grandfather of Jair (ver. 21) had married the daughter of Machir, of a noble house in the tribe of Manasseh, (Ch. 7: 14.) Therefore the same Jair is called the son of Manasseh, although he was only related to Manasseh by marriage."— See Def. Dic.

66. *The Father of Salah was Arphaxad.*—And Arphaxad lived five and thirty years and begat Salah.—Gen. 11: 12,

The Father of Sala was Cainan.—Which was the son of Sala, which was the son of Cainan, which was the son of Arphaxad. —Luke 3: 35, 36.

Some authors state that Cainan was the surname of Sala, and that the names should read thus: " The son of Heber which was the son of Salacainan, the son of Arphaxad." This is the more probable as the words *the son* are supplied by the translators in order to make it more intelligible to us, for the genealogies, as they stand in the Jewish records, are simply a series of names. Hence, the translator, who was unacquainted with the names, might easily make a division as above.

67.   *There were Fourteen Generations from Abraham to David.*—So all the generations from Abraham to David are fourteen generations.—Matt. 1: 17.

There were but Thirteen Generations from Abraham to David.—Abraham begat Isaac.........Jacob.........Judas.........Phares...... Esrom.........Aram.........Aminidab.........Naason.........Salmon......... Booz.........Obed.........Jesse.........David.........[13].—Matt. 1: 2-6.

Generation is a term applied either to a regular descent from father to son, or to a certain number of years. It is in this latter sense Matthew makes use of the word generation, " So all the generations from Abraham to David are fourteen generations," &c., not fourteen regular successions of father and sons; for he *proves* he never meant any such thing by giving, in the same paragraph, the names of a number of persons, sufficient to constitute the chain of progenitors up to Abraham, but not sufficient to make fourteen *progenitors* between David and Abraham. The term generation, even at the present day, is applied to a number of years.

In the English Court of Chancery, it has varied from sixty to twenty years. Among the Jews it has also varied from one hundred to thir-

ty years, so that the number of years constituting
the term *generation*, has varied at different peri-
ods of the world. Matthew took his account
from the Jewish records, and just copied what he
found therein recorded. Hence, the number of
years constituting fourteen generations, from
Abraham to David, was probably different from
the number of years constituting fourteen generations from David until the Babylonish captivity;
and again from the latter event to the coming of
Christ. Thus we find that so far from being any
evidence of error in Matthew's statement, the error is in the mind of the skeptic. See Dr. Sleigh.

**68. There were Fourteen Generations from the Babylonish
Captivity to Christ.**—And from the carrying away into Babylon unto
Christ are fourteen generations.—Matt. 1: 17

**There were but Thirteen Generations from the Babylonish
Captivity to Christ.**—And after they were brought to Babylon, Je-
chonias begat Salathiel.........Zerobabel.........Abiud......Eliakim......
Azor.........Sadoc.........Achim.........Eliud.........Eleazur.........Matthan
....Jacob.........Joseph, the husband of Mary, of whom was born
Jesus [13].—Matt. 1: 12, 16.

This has been explained under the foregoing
proposition. It is evident that Matthew's term
generations, signifies a certain number of years
which were recognized as generations, according
to the Hebrew standard.

69. The Infant Christ was taken into Egypt.—When he arose
he took the young child and his mother by night and departed into
Egypt, and was there until the death of Herod......... But when Herod was dead.........he took the young child and his mother and came
.........and dwelt in a city called Nazareth.—Matt. 1: 14, 15, 19, 23.

The Infant Christ was Not taken into Egypt.—And when the
days of her purification, according to the law of Moses, were accomplished, they brought him to Jerusalem, to present him to the Lord
.... And when they had performed all things, according to the law
of the Lord they returned.........to their own city, Nazareth.—Luke
2: 2¹, 29.

The skeptic's only difficulty on this point appears to be that he has got *his* chronology badly *mixed*. Luke writes on this subject of an event which took place a year previous to that recorded by Matthew. He says, " And when the days of her purification were accomplished (*i. e.* thirty three days, according to the law of Moses,) they brought him (the child) to Jerusalem to present him to the Lord, (please read the beautiful law recorded in Ex. 13: 2, Ex. 22: 29) and to offer a sacrifice according to that which is said in the law of the Lord —a pair of turtle doves or two young pigeons.— And when they had performed all things according to the law of the Lord, they returned into Gallilee—to their own city, Nazareth."

And according to the best chronology it was a year after this event, that Joseph being warned of God in a dream, took the young child and his mother by night and fled into Egypt, where they remained until the death of Herod.

Before leaving this subject we ought to remark, for the *information* (?) of the Infidel, that the events recorded in the Bible are not always *arranged* in the precise order in which they occurred. It is by no means necessary, in order for the Bible to be *true*, that all the events recorded by Matthew must chronologically *precede* those recorded by Mark and Luke. We see, therefore, in conclusion, that after the days of her (Mary's) purification, they returned to their own city Nazareth, and dwelt there a year, *after which* the infant Christ *was* taken into Egypt. Any ordinary mind can see the harmony between Matthew and Luke on this subject.

70. *Christ was Tempted in the Wilderness.*—And immediately [after Christ's baptism] the spirit driveth him into the wilderness.— And he was there in the wilderness forty days tempted of Satan.— Mark 1: 12, 13.

Christ was Not Tempted in the Wilderness.—And the third day [after Christ's baptism] there was a marriage in Cana of Galilee... .... Both Jesus was called and his disciples to the marriage.—John 2: 1, 2.

This *contradiction* (?) was manufactured by the three words *after Christ's baptism*, which has been inserted by the Infidel in the last text.— This statement inclosed in brackets is simply *false*. And had the skeptic read the previous chapter with any attention, he might have known it to be such, for it gives no account whatever of Christ's baptism.

The subjects of the chapter are, 1. The position and office of Christ, and, 2. The testimony of John that he *was-the Christ*, and this he proves by a statement of what occurred four years previous, when he immersed the Messiah in the Jordan.— And the next day after this, it appears he was with the same persons (or other unbelievers) again, for seeing Jesus coming unto him he said, " Behold the Lamb of God which taketh away the sin of the world," and adds, " This is he of whom I said, (at the time of the baptism, see Matt. 3: 11,) "After me cometh a man which is pre- ferred before me." He then continues his testi- mony with the words, " And I knew him not, but he that sent me to baptize with water, the same said unto me, Upon whom thou shalt see the Spirit descending and remaining upon him, the same is he which baptizeth with the Holy Ghost. And I saw and bare record that this is the Son of God."

In John 2: 1, we find the skeptic's quotation, " And on the third day there was a marriage in Cana of Galilee," &c. The third day after what? Not the third day after Christ's baptism as the In- fidel states, *for that took place four years previous* (as is easily seen by noticing the chronology at the head of the chapters) but the third day after the events recorded in the foregoing chapter, that is after John thus testifies to others that Jesus was the Christ, and proves his testimony by a statement of what he himself witnessed.

This proposition exhibits a dishonesty so bold and shameless that none but an Infidel would have the assurance to hold it up before a civilized world.

71. *Christ Preached His First Sermon on the Mount.*—And seeing the multitude he went up into a *mountain*, and when he was set his disciples came unto him. And he opened his mouth and taught them, saying.—Matt. 5: 1.

Christ Preached His First Sermon in the Plain.—And he came down with them and stood in the *plain*; and the company of his disciples, and a great multitude of people.........came to hear him......... And he lifted up his eyes on his disciples and said:—Luke 6: 7, 20.

This is another instance in which a direct falsehood has been ingeniously conveyed to the mind What authority has the Infidel for stating that the sermon which Christ delivered on the plain, as recorded in Luke 6: 17, 20, *was his first sermon?* What authority, indeed? What pretext or excuse can he have for this, when the very chapter preceding, gives an account of Christ preaching a sermon from Simon's ship, in the edge of Gennesaret, while his audience thronged the shore.— And in the chapter *next preceding this* we find the declaration, "And Jesus returned in the power of the spirit unto Galilee, and there went out the fame of him through all the regions round about, and he taught in their synagogues, being glorified of all." Luke 4: 14, 15. Immediately after this follows an account of a sermon in the synagogue at Nazareth. Again in verse 31 of the same chapter we read, "And (he) came down to Capernaum....and taught them on the Sabbath day," and when they urged him to stay with them, his reply, as recorded in verse 43, is, "I must preach the Kingdom of God in other cities, for therefore am I sent, and he preached in the synagogues of Galilee."

Yet in the very face of all these declarations in the two preceding chapters, when we come to the next instance recorded in Luke 6, the skeptic very coolly calls it *his first sermon!!* What beautiful consistency!! Had the Infidel taken the trouble to *read* the sermon delivered on the mount, (Matt. 5:) and the one delivered on the plain (Luke 6:) he would also have discovered *some* difference in the discourses.

72. *John was in Prison when Jesus went into Galilee.*—Now, after that John was put in prison Jesus came into *Galilee* preaching the gospel of the kingdom of God.—Mark 1: 14.

John was Not in Prison when Jesus went into Galilee.—The day following Jesus would go forth into *Galilee.*—John 1: 43. And after these things came Jesus with his disciples into the land of Judea......... And John was baptizing in Enon......... For John was *not yet* cast into prison.—John 3: 22, 23, 24.

This proposition is so arrayed as to convey to the mind the idea that Jesus never went into Galilee but *once*, whereas the Bible speaks of his being there some *seventeen times.* The green vales of Galilee were the witnesses of many of his noble deeds, and the clear waters of her beautiful lakes testify to his miracles and his love.

He went into Galilee many times *before* John was cast into prison, and many times *afterward.* Hence, the contradiction in the above proposition we fail to see.

73. *Christ's Disciples were Commanded to go forth with a Staff and Sandals.*—And commanded them that they should take nothing for their journey, save a *staff only*; no scrip, no bread, no money in their purse ; but be shod with sandals.—Mark 6: 8, 9.

Christ's Disciples are Commanded to go forth with Neither Staves nor Sandals.—Provide neither gold, nor silver, nor brass in your purses; nor scrip for your journey. neither two coats, neither shoes, nor yet staves.—Matt. 10: 9, 10.

Mark represents Jesus as telling his apostles to take nothing for their journey save a *staff* only, while in Matthew they are forbidden to take *staves;* there is nothing contradictory here, the evident idea of both texts is that they were to take *but one.* Probably one apiece, simply as an aid in walking, and not to carry several as if they designed thereby to protect themselves from physical harm. As they trusted in Omnipotence for protection they had no need to carry *staves* for weapons.

Also in Mark they are commanded to be shod with *sandals,* and in Matthew they are forbidden to provide themselves with *shoes;* but this is not inconsistent. The sandals were much lighter and more portable than shoes. The word sandal is purely Chaldee, and when translated means a light shoe. It is compounded of *sin* a shoe (see Targum, Deut. 25: 9, 10,) and *dal,* thin, light, slender, or mean, (see Martinus' Etymological Lexicon) they were much lighter than the *hypodema* or common shoe. Hence, in the commission, the preference was given to them. It is probable however, that our Savior intended more particularly to convey the idea that they were to take no change of garments, and this idea is sustained by Wilson's version of Matt. 10: 9, 10, which reads thus, "Carry no traveling bag, no spare clothes, shoes, or staff." See Emphatic Diaglott.

74. *A Woman of Canaan Besought Jesus.*—And behold, a woman of *Canaan* came out of the same coasts, and cried unto him, Have mercy on me, O Lord, thou son of David; my daughter is grievously vexed with a devil.--Matt. 15: 22.

It was a Greek Woman who Besought Him.—The woman was

a *Greek*, a *Syrophenician* by nation, and she besought him that he would cast forth the devil out of her daughter.—Mark 7: 26.

Syrophenicia was in the time of our Saviour a province of the Greek government, and was inhabited by the descendents of Canaan. The woman referred to in the above proposition, lived in Syrophenicia, hence she was a Greek, and as she was descended from Canaan, she was also "a woman of Canaan." Thus we may speak of a negro who was born in Kentucky, and say of him with equal propriety, that he is a "man of Africa," an "American" and a "Kentuckian." Hence we see that the Bible is in perfect harmony on this, as well as all other points.

75. *Two Blind Men Besought Jesus.*—And behold, *two blind men* sitting by the way-side, when they heard that Jesus passed by, cried out, saying, Have mercy on us, O Lord thou son of David.—Matt. 20: 30.

Only ONE Blind Man Besought Him.—A certain *blind man* sat by the way-side begging......... And he cried, saying, Jesus, thou son of David, have mercy on me.—Luke 18: 35, 38

Had the infidel quoted the context in the above, his proposition would have beautifully explained itself. We give the sense entire.— Luke says, "And it came to pass as they came nigh unto Jericho, a certain blind man sat by the wayside begging. And hearing the multitude pass by, he asked what it meant. And they told him Jesus of Nazareth passeth by. And he cried saying, "Jesus, thou Son of David, have mercy on me.'

And Matt. says, "And as they departed from Jericho, a great multitude followed him. And behold *two* blind men sitting by the wayside, and when they heard that Jesus passed by, cried out saying, Have mercy upon us, Oh Lord, thou Son of David." Hence it is clear that Luke and Matthew refer to *two* distinct and separate instances, one of which took place before Jesus and his disciples arrived at Jericho, and the other *after* they departed from thence

76.   *Christ was Crucified at the THIRD Hour.*—And it was the *third hour* and they crucified him.—Mark 15: 25.

Christ was not Crucified until the SIXTH Hour.--And it was the preparation of the passover, and about the *sixth hour*; and he saith unto the Jews, Behold your king........., Shall I crucify your king.—John 19: 14, 15.

It is supposed that the true reading of John 19 : 14 should be *trite*, the third, instead of *exte* the sixth.   A mistake which might readily have occurred in ancient times when the character *gamma*, which was used to denote *trite* three, might be mistaken for *episima*, or *sigma tau*, which signifies six.

The two characters above alluded to are very much alike, hence the mistake was easy.   Thus we see that which the critic supposed to be a mistake on the part of the *author of the Bible* was simply a mistake made by a few of those who copied the work, we say a *few*, because *trite* third (instead of *exte* six) is the reading of some very eminent manuscripts.   See Dr. Clark, Bengel, Newcome, McKnight, Lightfoot, Rosenmuller, &c., on this point.

77.   *The TWO THIEVES Reviled Christ.*--The *thieves* also, which were crucified with him, cast the same in his teeth,--Matt. 27: 44.   And *they* that were crucified reviled him.--Mark 15: 32.

Only ONE of THE THIEVES Reviled Christ.—And *one* of the malefactors which hanged railed on him......... But the other answering, rebuked him, saying, Dost thou not fear God, seeing thou art in the same condemnation ?--Luke 23: 39, 40.

It is plain from the three texts above quoted

that at first (according to Matthew and Mark) both of the thieves reviled the Messiah, and afterward (according to Luke,) one had not only ceased to revile him, but reproved the other for so doing. Hence the infidel argues with great complacency, "the Bible contradicts itself."— Surely this is a very weak argument for a man to offer, and that too, in the very face of the fact that they hung over six hours upon the cross.— Saul of Tarsus and many others were converted in much less time than this.

78. Satan ENTERED into Judas While at THE SUPPER. —And after the sop Satan entered into him.—John 13: 27.

Satan ENTERED into him BEFORE THE SUPPER.— Then entered Satan into Judas,.........and he went his way and communed with the chief priests and captains, how he might betray him......... *Then came the day* of unleavened bread when the passover must be killed.--Luke 22: 3, 4, 7.

We are weary of correcting propositions which are so transparent as to need no solution. From the above it is evident that Satan entered into Judas *twice.* Once when he consented to betray his Lord for money, and again " after the supper " to strengthen him in his purpose to deliver up his master to those who thirsted for his blood.

79. Judas Committed SUICIDE by Hanging.—And he cast down the pieces of silver into the temple, and departed, and went out and hanged himself.—Matt. 27: 5.

. Judas did NOT HANG Himself, but Died another way.— And falling headlong he burst asunder in the midst, and all his *bowels gushed out.*--Acts 1: 18.

It is written in Matt. 27: 5 that Judas went and hanged himself. Luke in Acts 1: 18 relates these circumstances only which followed *after* he had hanged himself; viz: that " falling headlong" (perhaps by the rope breaking, or that to which he had fastened it giving way,) " he burst assunder in the midst and all his bowels gushed out." There is no knowing how long (perhaps weeks, or even months) he might have remained suspended (for it is probable that he hung himself in some unfrequented part of the neighboring woods) even until decomposition of his body had far advanced, and then falling from a very low height indeed would be quite sufficient to cause a rupture or bursting of the parietes of the abdomen and the consequent gushing out of his intestines or bowels.

80. THE POTTER'S FIELD was PURCHASED by JUDAS.--Now, this man purchased a field with the reward of iniquity. —Acts 1: 19.

THE POTTER'S FIELD was PURCHASED by THE CHIEF PRIESTS.--And the chief priests took the silver pieces ....and bought with them the potter's field.--Matt. 27: 6. 7.

" Now this man purchased a field with the reward of iniquity." Upon examination we find that this text, and also the one recorded in Matthew are literally true, for *the reward of iniquity* (*i. e.* of Judas' iniquity) bought the potter's field ; consequently it was Judas, who, by his iniquity in betraying his Lord and master, actually bought this property, although it was the priests who handed over the money for the field to its owners ; they were the agents, he was the principal. As it may be said of any rich man, he purchased such a piece of ground, although he may never have seen either the land nor its owners, yet it may be truthfully said of him, that he bought the property if it was done with his money, while another person in speaking of the same transaction could also say with truth, that the land was purchased by the agent who transacted the business.

81. But ONE Woman came to the SEPULCHRE.—The first day of the week cometh Mary Magdalene, early, when it was yet dark, unto the sepulchre.—John 20: 1.

TWO Women came to the SEPULCHRE.—In the end of the Sabbath, as it began to dawn towards the first day of the week, came Mary Magdalene, and the OTHER MARY to the sepulchre.—Matt. 28: 1.

John simply mentions Mary Magdelene as coming early unto the sepulchre; he does not say that she came alone, (as he would be obliged to do in order to sustain the skeptic's position.)—There might have been other women with her, without invalidating in the least, John's statement *that she came.*

Matthew corroborates John's testimony that Mary Magdalene came to the sepulchre, and adds that the other Mary was with her. Hence, instead of contradicting John, he bears witness that his record is true.

82. THREE WOMEN CAME to the SEPULCHRE.—When the Sabbath was past, Mary Magdalene, and Mary the mother of James, and Salome, had brought sweet spices, that they might come and anoint him.—Mark 16: 1.

MORE THAN THREE WOMEN came to the SEPULCHRE.—It was Mary Magdalene and Mary the Mother of James, and OTHER WOMEN that were with them.—Luke 24: 10.

This is similar to the preceding objection.—Mark testifies that both Matthew and John told the truth in the previous proposition, and adds that Salome was also with them. Luke declares that the three preceding witnesses are correct, in relation to the women which they have specified, and conveys the idea that there were quite a number of them. So there is no discrepency here. John merely thought proper to mention Mary Magdalene, she being the most prominent and foremost of the group, while the other Evangelist casually mention a few of those that were with her, some more and some less. There may have been many women with Mary Magdalene, on that memorable morning without invalidating the testimony of either of the Evangelists.

83. *It was at Sunrise when they came to the Sepulchre.*— And very early in the morning, the first day of the week, they came unto the sepulchre, at the *rising of the sun.*—Mark 16: 2.

It was SOME TIME BEFORE sunrise when they came. The first day of the week, cometh Mary Magdalene, early, *while it was yet dark,* unto the sepulchre.—John 20 : 1.

The grammar of the language gives the solution to this problem, for John says "while it was yet dark *cometh* Mary Magdalene," &c., which shows clearly that she was on her way, coming to the sepulchre, while it was yet dark.— And in accordance with this, Mark testifies that they came unto the sepulchre, at the rising of the sun.

Hence, it is clear that they left their homes very early, while it was yet dark, and arrived at the tomb at sunrise. When the skeptic is so *very* particular about the precise hour in the morning, it might be well for him to pay some attention to the tense of the verbs with which he has to deal.

Before leaving this subject we will state that Wakefield's translation fully sustains the above position. His version of John 20: 1, is as follows: " Now on the first day of the week, Mary Magdalene *setteth out* early in the morning, while it was yet dark, *towards* the tomb."

The word which is rendered *cometh* in our version, is the Greek word *Erketai*, being the present tense of the verb *Erkomai*, which Groves, in his Greek Lexicon, defines thus: " To issue, come forth, arise from," &c. Hence the literal reading of *Erketai* is *issuing, coming forth, arising from.*" Hence we learn that early in the morning, while it was yet dark, Mary Magdalene was *coming forth,* or *arising from* her home, to go towards the sepulchre of her Lord.

4

84. *Two Angels-were seen at the Sepulchre, standing up.*
—And it came to pass, as they were much perplexed thereabout,
behold, *two* men *stood* by them in shining garments.—Luke 24: 4.

But ONE angel was seen and he was SITTING DOWN.—
For the angel of the Lord descended from heaven, and came and
rolled back the stone from the door, and *sat* upon it.........And the
angel answered and said unto the women, Fear not.—Matt. 28: 2, 5.

We can see no discrepancy between these two
texts. Matthew gives an account of the glorious
phenomenon of the resurrection. He speaks of
the earthquake that rent the rocks—of the glory-
clad messenger of Jehovah who rolled the stone
away from the tomb—the fear of the Roman
guards, and adds "The Angel answered and said
unto the women, Fear not ye, for I know that ye
seek Jesus that was crucified; he is not here for
he is risen, as he said; Come, see the place where
the Lord lay."

Luke here takes up the narration and gives an
account of what they saw *inside* of the sepulchre,
after they had entered, *in compliance with the in-
vitation of the angel* who sat upon the stone
which he had rolled away from the mouth of the
tomb. He says, "And they *entered in* and found
not the body of the Lord Jesus. And it came to
pass....behold *two men* stood by them." We
would ask the infidel, in all candor, *Where is the
inconsistency?*

It is evident from the two accounts that they
found the angel sitting on the stone near the mouth
of the tomb. He invites them to enter and
"see where the Lord lay," (*i. e.* had lain.) His
language is "*Come* and see." He may have
changed his position and escorted them to the
tomb. He may even have entered with them.—
He himself may have been one of the two angels
seen inside. His language, "*Come*," would justify the idea; but it matters not for the veracity
of either evangelist, whether he changed his po-

sition at all or not. As the women approached the sepulchre, he was nearer the tomb than they, therefore he could with perfect propriety ' say, " *Come* and see." Suffice it to say, the women saw him upon the outside, and he invited them to enter the tomb, and when they had entered, they saw two angels inside. The fact is as simple as the alphabet, and as clear as noonday. Truth shines in every sentence; and yet out of the statement, the skeptic has manufactured a proposition, which he expects to palm off upon the world, as a " *self-contradiction of the Bible.*"

85. *Two Angels were seen within the Sepulchre.*—And as she wept she stooped down and looked into the sepulchre, and seeth *two angels* in white.—John 20: 11, 12.

But ONE Angel was seen within the Sepulchre.—And entering into the sepulchre, they saw a young man sitting on the right side, clothed in a long white garment.—Mark 16: 5,

There is no difficulty in these texts, when we learn by the connection that the incidents occurred at two different visits to the sepulchre. Mark is speaking of the first, and of what the women saw inside, and in doing so he only mentions the angel who *spoke*, thereby making himself more prominent than his companion.

And John records Mary's *second* visit, after the other women had gone, and also the disciples, and while she stood there weeping "she stooped down and looked into the sepulchre, and seeth two angels in white," &c. Hence we see that the entire narration is consistent with itself, although it is given in parts, frequently disconnected and by four different individuals.

86. *Christ was to be three days and three nights in the grave.*—So shall the Son of Man be *three days* and *three nights* in the heart of the earth.—Matt. 12: 40.

Christ was but TWO days and TWO nights in the grave.— And it was the third hour, and they crucified him.........It was the preparation, that is, the *day before the Sabbath*.........And Pilate ....gave the body to Joseph. And he.........laid him in a sepulchre ....Now, when Jesus was risen *early* the *first day of the week*, he appeared first to Mary Magdalene.—Mark 15: 25, 42, 44, 45, 46. Mark 16: 9.

The expression used in Matt. 12: 40, is merely a synecdoche, or a phrase wherin a part is spoken of as the whole. " Day and night" was a common term amongst the Jews, applied in the reckoning of time to *a day* or to *any part* of a day.— Thus, as Jonah was three days and three nights in the fish, so was the son of man to be in the earth. That is, simply three days, *not seventy-two hours*. Thus he was swallowed by the fish on one day (day and night), remained in the fish the second, and was discharged from it the third day. Hence it may be said that he was three days and three nights (a part of three days) in the fish.— The same mode of expression is adopted even in our own times on many occasions ; for instance, there are three days of grace on bills of exchange, that is, of course, twenty-four hours for each day. The bill becomes due on the fifth of the month, and the three days of grace expire on the seventh, so there is actually but *one whole day*, and only a part of two days.

In Gen 1: the evening and the morning (night and day) are no less than six times called simply " day." And again in Gen. 7: 17, the term forty days is used for forty days and forty nights.— Lastly, the transaction mentioned in Esther 4: 16, and Esther 5: 1, proves beyond all dispute, that the expression, *day and night*, merely meant what we call *day*. There it is recorded that Esther and the Jews fasted *three days* and *three nights*. And this, although the day on which the command was given is included, and the third day, the day of the banquet (ver. 4) is also included, so that in fact there was but *one* whole day, or a part of two days and two nights, and yet that period is called three days and three nights, which simply implies three days or even parts of days. See Dr. Sleigh.

87. *The Holy Ghost bestowed at Pentecost.*—But ye shall re-ceive power after that the Holy Ghost is come upon you......Ye shall be baptized with the Holy Ghost *not* many days hence.—Acts 1: 8, 5, And when the day of Pentecost was fully come they were all of one accord in one place......And they were all filled with the Holy Ghost. —Acts 1; 4.

The Holy Ghost bestowed BEFORE Pentecost.—And when he had said this he breathed on them, and said unto them, Receive ye the Holy Ghost.—John 20: 22.

The words, "Receive ye the Holy Ghost," contain a *promise* that it shall be bestowed, but it does not specify any time when it shall be given. And, although the disciples had the promise of the Holy Ghost, they did not *expect* it previous to the ascension of the Messiah, for Jesus distinct-ly tells them that "If I go not away, the Com-forter (or Holy Ghost) will not come."

88. *The Disciples were commanded immediately after the Resurrection to go into Galilee.*—Then said Jesus unto them, Be not afraid ; go tell my brethren that they *go* into Galilee, and there shall they see me.—Matt. 28: 10.

The Disciples were commanded immediately after the Res-urrection to TARRY AT JERUSALEM.—But *tarry* ye in Je-rusalem until ye be endued with power from on high.—Lu. 24: 49.

The command "Tarry ye in Jerusalem until ye be endued with power from on high," was *not* given *immediately after* the resurrection, as the skeptic distinctly states, but after Jesus had tar-ried with his disciples *for forty days ;* it was the very last charge he gave them before his ascen-sion! Is it ignorance, worse than that which characterized the dark ages, or willful falsehood, which we are thus called upon to expose ?

89. Jesus first appeared to the eleven disciples in a room at Jerusalem.—And they rose up the same hour and returned to Jerusalem, and found the eleven gathered together.........And as they spake, Jesus himself stood in the midst of them.........But they were terrified and affrighted, and supposed that they had seen a spirit.—Luke 24: 33, 36, 37. The same day, at evening, being the first day of the week, when the doors were shut, where the disciples were assembled.........came Jesus and stood in the midst.—John 20: 19.

Jesus first appeared to the Eleven on a MOUNTAIN in GALILEE.—Then the eleven disciples went away into Galilee, unto a mountain where Jesus had appointed. And when they saw him they worshipped him, but some doubted.—Matt. 28: 16, 17.

There is surely no discrepancy here. It is evident from the reading of the Word, that the meeting in Jerusalem was *previous* to the one in Galilee. On the same night after his resurrection, his disciples were voluntarily gathered together in Jerusalem (previous to going into Galilee) and the Lord appeared unto them. Luke 24: is a very comprehensive chapter—it embraces a period of forty days, or the whole time from the resurrection to the ascension of our Lord, and in consequence of its brevity, many things are necessarily omitted, and among them we find the meeting of Jesus with his disciples on the mount in Galilee, according to previous appointment.— This elipsis is filled by Matthew, but because one evangelist records what another omits, is certainly *no proof* that the Bible contradicts itself. And, although it is evident from the connection that the meeting in Jerusalem was the first one, after his resurrection, it is well to observe that neither of them is called the *first meeting* in the text.

90. Christ ascended from Mount Olivet.—And when he had spoken these things, while they beheld, he was taken up, and a cloud received him out of their sight.........Then returned they unto Jerusalem, from the mount called *Olivet.*—Acts 1: 9, 12.

Christ ascended from BETHANY.—And he led them out as far as to *Bethany*; and he lifted up his hands and blessed them.— And it came to pass that while he blessed them, he was parted from them, and carried up into heaven.—Luke 24: 50, 51.

Modern skeptics of small intellect, and less in-formation, have said a great deal about the two texts above quoted. We have read about this "dreadful contradiction, so fatal to the veracity of the sacred writers," and they ask, with all the sarcasm of conceited ignorance, "Which tells the truth?" Shall we believe Luke, or the statement found in Acts?" To which we reply, believe them *both.* Allow us to state, for the information of this class of second-rate infidels, that "Bethany was a village which was built on the south-east side of the mount of Olives. See Mark 11: 1, also Bible Dictionary, Encyclopedia, &c. Hence, the difficulty at once vanishes, and we find that a little knowledge of geography would not be out of place in the infidel's brain. Suppose an au-thor in writing the life of George Washington, should say in one place that he died at Mount Vernon, and again that he died in Virginia—if a man should attempt to prove that in making these two statements, the author contradicted himself, the civilized world would at once pronounce him either a lunatic or a fool, and yet in the above proposition, the compiler places himself in the same position.

91. *Paul's attendants heard the miraculous voice, and stood speechless.*—And the men which journeyed with [Paul] *stood speechless, hearing a voice* but seeing no man.—Acts 9: 7.

Paul's attendants heard NOT the voice, and were Prostrate.—And they that were with me saw indeed the light and were afraid; but they *heard not* the voice of him that spake to me.—Acts 22: 9. And when we were *all fallen to the earth,* I heard a voice.—Acts 26 : 14.

A little investigation reveals the simple truth and harmony of this apparent discrepancy. The verb "to hear," is repeatedly used, not only in the Scriptures, but also in common conversation, to signify, not merely the hearing of a voice, (or sound,) but the *understanding*, or *obeying it*; for instance, the Lord Jesus said to those who heard him, " He that hath ears to hear, let him hear," (or understand.) Again, he that heareth you, (the Apostles,) heareth (or obeyeth) me.— And people often say to a stubborn or stupid child, "Do you hear me?" That is, do you understand me? or will you obey me? The case mentioned above is simply this: In the first instance, the narrator states that the men who accompanied Paul, heard a *voice*, that is, were merely sensible that some one spoke: whereas in the second instance, Paul declares they *heard* not the voice of him that spake unto him, (Paul,) that is they comprehended not its meaning, or understood not what was said. And this explanation is fully sustained by some of our best modern translations, among which we may mention— "The Diaglott," "The Improved Version," and "Wakefield." In relation to the *position* of the parties, it is easy to see that in this connection, the words "stood speechless," merely indicate a *condition*, and have no reference to *posture*. As man may stand *speechless*, stand in *doubt*, stand in *fear*, stand *firm*, or stand *in awe*, and at the same time choose any position of body he pleases. He may be sitting, or standing, or lying down, without impeaching the veracity of the narrator, who speaks of him as being in these conditions. It is clear that in the text above referred to, the words, "stood speechless," simply imply a condition of of dumbness, and convey the same idea as if the author had said they *remained* speechless, or remained silent.

92. *Abraham departed to go into Canaan.*—And Abram took Sarah his wife, and Lot, his brother's son.........and they went forth to go into the land of Canaan, and into the land of Canaan they came.—Gen. 12: 5,

Abraham went, not knowing where.—By faith Abraham when he was called to go out into a place which he should after receive for an inheritance, obeyed; and he went out not knowing whither he went.—Heb. 11 : 8.

There is not a *shadow* of inconsistency here.— The Lord called upon Abraham to leave his country, his kindred, and his father's house, and go into a land which he promised to show unto him. " So Abraham departed, as the Lord had spoken unto him." He implicitly believed the words of Jehovah, and "went out, not knowing whither he went;" but the Lord led him on, until he came into the land of Canaan, and *then* " the Lord appeared unto Abraham and said, unto thy seed will I give *this* land ; and there builded he an altar unto the Lord who appeared unto him." If Abraham *knew* when he went forth, that it was the land of Canaan which the Lord designed to give him, (as the skeptic basely insinuates,) why was it necessary for the Lord to appear to him on his arrival there, and tell him that which he knew already ?

We are weary of explaining propositions like the above, which are so simple that they *need* no solution, and were it not that the little work before us is considered the "strong tower" of infidelity, we should have thrown it aside long since, in disgust.

93. *Abraham had Two Sons.*—Abraham had two sons; the one by a bond-woman, and the other by a free woman.—Gal. 4: 22.

Abraham had but ONE son.—By faith Abraham when he was tried, offered up Isaac,.........his only begotten son.—Heb, 11 : 17.

The only difficulty in this proposition, is in the text in Heb., where Isaac is spoken of as the only begotten son of Abraham, while the patriarch was the father of another child, according to the flesh. But this apparent obscurity of expres-

sion, is at once removed, by a careful reading of
the text and its connections. Please notice.—
" By faith, Abraham, when he was tried, offered
up Isaac; and he that had received the promises,
offered up his only begotten son, of whom it was
said, that in *Isaac* shall thy seed be called."—
Hence we see at once that the text does not say
that Isaac was the *only* son of Abraham, but that
he was the " only begotten son *of whom* (or *concerning* whom, according to Dr. Doddrige,) it was
said, That in Isaac shall thy seed be called."—
Still, Isaac might very properly be called the only
begotten son, in a *legal* point of view, as he was
the only child of Abraham's lawful wife, the heir
of his father's property, and the heir of God's
promises to Abraham's seed.

94. *Keturah was Abraham's wife.*—Then again Abraham took
a wife, and her name was Keturah.—Gen. 25 : 1.

Keturah was Abraham's CONCUBINE.—The sons of Keturah
Abraham's concubine.—1 Chron. 1: 32.

The boasted " contradiction " between these
two texts, vanishes like dew before the sun, when
exposed to the candid light of honest investigation. A close examination of Gen. 25: 1, explains the matter clearly, for the word that is here
rendered " wife," is in the Hebrew " *ashaw*,"
and its primary definition, as given by Gesenius
is " A woman, female of any age or condition,
married or unmarried. It is used in Cant. 1: 8,
in the expression, "O thou fairest among women."
It is applied to unmarried females, in Gen. 24: 5,
also in Isa. 4: 1. It is used as the name of the
sex, and is thus applied to animals, to denote the
female, in Gen. 1: 2. Frequent in the phrase
" *lakah lo leashaw*," to take to one's self a woman
for a wife. See Gen. 4: 19, 6: 2. Spoken also of
a *concubine* in Gen. 30: 4, and in Judges. It is

also a term of reproach for a man who is weak, cowardly, or effeminate, as in Isa. 19: 16; Isa. 3: 12; Jer. 51: 30; also Nah. 3: 13.* This being the definition of the word, as given by the best authority we have, the text ceases to present even the semblance of a contradiction to 1 Chron. 1: 32. Even admitting that the word *ashaw* denotes a *wife*, in the above connection, the difficulty is obviated by a critical definition of the word *concubine*. It is thus defined by Webster: "a wife of inferior condition; a *lawful* wife, but not united to the man by the usual ceremonies, and of inferior condition. Such were Hagar and Keturah, the concubines of Abraham, and such concubines were allowed by the Roman laws." See Webster's Unabridged Dictionary. Hence the infidel's case is rendered hopeless, by the light of truth.

95. *Abraham begat a son when he was a hundred years old, by the interposition of Providence.*—Sarah conceived and bare Abraham a son in his *old age*, at the set time of which God had spoken to him.—Gen. 21: 2. And being not weak in the faith, he considered not his own body, now *dead*, when he was a hundred years old.—Rom. 4: 19. Therefore sprang there even from one, and him *as good as dead*, so many as the stars of the sky.—Heb. 11: 12.

Abraham begat SIX children more, after he was a hundred years old, WITHOUT any interposition of Providence.—Then again Abraham took a wife and her name was Keturah; and she bare him Zimram, and Jokshan, and Medan, and Midian, and Ishbak, and Shuah.—Gen. 25: 1, 2.

The skeptic does not even *claim* a contradiction here. Hence we have nothing to do. It was evidently inserted in the series before us, simply to make the number complete. His proposition in itself, does not present even a *semblance* of discrepancy. He says, "Abraham begat a son,

*See Gesenius' Hebrew Lexicon, page 92 and 93.

when he was a hundred years old, by the interposition of Providence," in which statement he is
well sustained by the inspired record. He also
says that "Abraham begat *six children more*, after he was a hundred years old," &c., &c. Well,
what of it? Where is the contradiction? It is
not even surprising as a physiological fact, that he
should become the father of other children, after
his youthful vigor had been miraculously restored.

We have found many propositions before this,
which were weak enough to excite either our pity
or contempt, but this is surely the most insipid
objection to the veracity of Bible writers, that we
have ever seen. What a system must infidelity
be, when its votaries are driven to such foolish
and contemptible objections to God's word, in order to maintain its very existence.

96. *Jacob bought a sepulchre from Hamor.*—And the bones of
Joseph.........buried they in Shechem, in a parcel of ground which
Jacob bought of the sons of Hamor, the father of Shechem.—
Josh. 24 : 32.

***ABRAHAM bought it of Hamor.*—**In the sepulchre that Abra-
ham bought for a sum of money of the sons of Emmor, the father
of Sychem.—Acts 7: 16.

We have the statement here quoted, that Jacob
bought "a parcel of ground," of the sons of
Hamor, the father of Shechem, and again that
Abraham bought a sepulchre of the same party.
And because the *field* which Jacob bought was used
as a burial place, the infidel endeavors to make
it appear that it was *identical* with the *sepulchre*
purchased by Abraham. One man bought a *field*
and the other a *sepulchre*, but they were purchased from the same party, therefore the skeptic eagerly exclaims, "*the Bible contradicts itself.*'—
This is evidently a very satisfactory conclusion for
him to come to, but the mode of reasoning which

he adopts is, to say the least, a little *peculiar.*— The fact that two different parties make a purchase of land from the same individual, certainly does not indicate that they both bought the same piece of property. It is probable that Jacob bought the field surrounding the sepulchre, purchased by Abraham, thereby *enlarging* the burial-place of his fathers'. Still, the two pieces of property may have been many miles apart, without impeaching in the least, the veracity of the sacred writer.

97. *God promised the land of Canaan to Abraham and his seed forever.*—And the Lord said unto Abraham, after Lot was separated from him. Lift up now thine eyes and look from the place where thou art, northward and southward, and eastward and westward; for *all the land* which thou seest, to thee will I give it and to thy seed *forever*.........For I will give it unto thee.........Unto thee and thy seed after thee.—Gen. 13 : 14, 15, 17; Gen. 17 : 8.

Abraham and his seed never received the promised land.— And he gave him [Abraham] none inheritance in it, no, not so much as to set his foot on.—Acts 7 : 15. By faith he sojourned in the land of promise as in a strange country, dwelling in tents with Isaac and Jacob, the heirs with him of the same promise.........These all died in faith, not having received the promises.—Heb. 11: 9, 13.

It is clear from the covenant which God made with Abraham, that he was to inherit the land of Canaan forever. God assures him that he will give him all the land between the two great rivers Egypt and Euphrates, for an *everlasting possession*, and he not only promised this land to Abraham, but to Christ, as his seed. For Paul says, "To Abraham and his seed were the promises made. He saith not, And to seeds, as of many; but as of one, And to thy seed, which is Christ." Gal. 3:16. Christ then was a party to the covenant, and must inherit the land with Abraham, forever. The infidel, however, finds what he claims to be a mistake, from the fact that Abraham did not receive the promised inheritance before his death. But the promise standeth sure, it is still gleaming in the temple of truth, and eternity will vindicate the justice and veracity of Jehovah. The patriarch *did not expect* to receive the promised possesion in his natural life time; a mortal man could not receive an *everlasting* inheritance.

Paul says of Abraham, Isaac and Jacob, that they "died in the *faith*, not having received the promises, but having seen them afar off, were persuaded of them and embraced them, and confessed that they were pilgrims and strangers." They were looking on beyond the resurrection of God's sleeping children—beyond the second coming of Jesus, to the age of millennial glory, when Messiah shall reign from sea to sea, and from the rivers to the ends of the earth. Then shall the ancient worthies stand upon the glorified hill-tops of a purified earth, and walk beside the crystal streams of Eden restored. The crown of immortal youth shall rest upon their brows and they shall receive the inheritance which was promised to Abraham and his seed for an everlasting possession. Where "the kingdom is the Lord's and he is the governor among the nations." A skeptic's eye can never reach the glories of the promised land, his mind can never appreciate the loveliness of a new born earth, where every knee shall bow and every tongue confess the glory of the Lord.

God never indicated to Abraham that he was to receive the inheritance during his natural life time, but the patriarch looked forward with joyful anticipation to the time when there should be given to the Son of man, dominion and glory, and a kingdom, that all people, nations and languages should serve him; for his dominion shall be an everlasting dominion, and his kingdom that which shall not be destroyed. Then instead of the thorn, shall come up the fir-tree, instead of the brier, shall come up the myrtle-tree. Please see Dan. 7: 13, 14, 27; Ps. 22: 27, 28; Rev. 5: 10; Matt. 19: 28; Luke 1: 31: 32; Rev. 20: 4, 6; Ps. 2: 6, 10; Matt. 5: 5; Rev. 11: 15.

98. *Goliath was slain by Elhanan.*—And there was again a battle in Gob with the Philistines, where Elhanan the son of Jaare-oregim a Bethlehemite, slew ["the brother of." supplied by the translators] Goliath the Gittite, the staff of whose spear was like a weaver's beam.—2 Sam. 21 : 19.

The BROTHER of Goliath was slain by Elhanan.—And there was war again with the Philistines, and Elhanan the son of Jair slew Lahmi the brother of Goliath the Gittite, whose spear's staff was like a weaver's beam.—1 Chron. 20 : 5

The variation in the two texts above quoted, is easily accounted for, by considering that "*ore-gim,*" which signifies *weavers*, has slipped out of one line into the other, and that "*Beth ha lachmi,*" the Bethlemite, is corrupted from "*eth lachmi,*" (Lahmi, the brother,) then the reading will be the same as in Chronicles. Dr. Kennicott has made this appear very plain in his first dissertation on the Hebrew text, page 78. Hence it will be seen that what the infidel supposes to be a mistake of inspiration, was merely the oversight of a transcriber, and surely no one claims that either the transcribers or translators of the Bible, were either inspired or infallible. We would remark further, that although the variation may be easily accounted for as above, and the texts harmonized upon the idea that the same giant is referred to in both places, still it does not necessarily follow that this is the case. For the Goliath which David slew, had four sons, all of whom were giants, and bore the family name of their father. (See Winer.)— And it is not at all unlikely that Elhanan, a chief in David's army, may have slain more than one

of them in battle.   We can see no inconsistency
between the statement that he slew " Goliath the
Gittite," and the declaration that "Lahmi, the
brother of Goliath the Gittite," fell also by his
hand.

99. Ahaziah began to reign in the twelfth year of Joram.—
In the twelfth year of Joram, the son of Ahab, king of Israel, did
Ahaziah the son of Jehoram king of Judah begin to reign.—2
Kings, 8 : 25.

*Ahaziah Began to reign in the **ELEVENTH** year of Joram.*
In the eleventh year of Joram the son of Ahab began Ahaziah to
reign over Judah.—2 Kings, 9 : 29.

The note in our margin contains as good an
account of this chronological difficulty, as can be
reasonably required.   Then he began to reign as
viceroy to his father, in his sickness.   2 Chron.
21: 18, 19.   But in Joram's twelfth year he began
to reign alone.   2 Chron. 8: 26.   See Dr. Clarke.

100. Michal had no child.—Therefore Michal the daughter of
Saul, had no child unto the day of her death.—2 Sam. 6: 23,

Michal had five children.—The five sons of Michal the daughter
of Saul.—2 Sam. 21 ; 8.

The marginal reading solves this problem also.
It explains the text in 2 Sam. 21: 8, as follows :
"The five sons of Michal's *sister*, the daughter
of Saul."   It is evident, that after the death of
her sister Michal took her five sons " whom she
brought up for Adriel," (the father of the children.)   Two of Dr. Kennicott's manuscripts have
Merab, the *sister* of Michal, not Michal, the
Chaldee has properly Merab, but it renders the
passage thus: "And the five sons of Merab,
which Michal, the daughter of Saul brought up."
With this view, the whole difficulty vanishes at
once.   We have not, in this harmony, claimed in-

fallibility for the King's translation. All we have proposed to do, was to show that one Bible wri ter has not contradicted another, or crossed himself.

101. *David was tempted by the Lord to number Israel.*—And the anger of the Lord was kindled against Israel, and he moved David against them to say, Go number Israel and Judah.—2 Sam. 24: 1.

David was tempted by SATAN to number the people.—And Satan stood up against Israel and provoked David to number Israel.—1 Chr. 21 : 1.

The apparent contradiction between these two texts, arises from inferring that the pronoun "he," in 2 Sam. 24: 1, refers to Jehovah, instead of Satan, whom we are informed in the other passage, was the tempter. The antecedent of the pronoun "he," is found in the margin, which reads "Satan." Dr. Boothroyd, renders the text, "The anger of the Lord was excited against Israel, because an adversary stood up and moved David, &c.—Jehovah's displeasure was evidently the *effect*, not the *cause*, of this numbering of Israel, which Satan induced David to do, preparatory doubtless, to engaging in some new contest, which his ambition had in view.

102. *The number of fighting men of Israel was 800,000 ; and of Judah 500,000.*—And Joab gave up the sum of the number of the people unto the king : and there were in Israel eight hundred thousand valiant men that drew the sword : and the men of Judah five hundred thousand men.—2 Sam. 24: 9.

The number of fighting men of Israel was 1,100,000 ; and of Judah 470,000.—And Joab gave the sum of the number of the people unto David. And all they of Israel were a thousand thousand and a hundred thousand [1,100,000] men that drew the sword ; and Judah was four hundred three score and ten thousand [470,000] men that drew the sword.—1 Chron. 21: 5.

It is written in 2 Sam. 24: 9, that "there were in Israel eight hundred thousand valiant men that drew the sword; and men of Judah five hundred thousand," but in Chron. we find "the number of Israel were eleven hundred thousand; and Judah four hundred three score and ten thousand," making, to all appearance, a difference of *three hundred thousand* Israelites, and *thirty thousand* Benjaminites. But it appears from Chronicles that there were twelve divisions of generals, who commanded monthly, and whose duty it was to keep guard near the king's person, each having a body of troops consisting of twenty-four thousand men, which jointly formed a grand army of two hundred and eighty-eight thousand; and as a separate body of twelve thousand men attended on the twelve princes of the twelve tribes, mentioned in the same chapter, the whole makes *three hundred thousand*, which is just the difference between the two accounts of eight hundred thousand, and of one million one hundred thousand. And here we have found the natural solution of the difficulty.

As to the men in Israel, the author of Samuel does not take notice of the three hundred thousand, because they were in the actual service of the king as a standing army, and therefore there was no need of numbering them; but in Chronicles they are joined to the rest, saying expressly, " *all those* of Israel were one million one hundred thousand." But in Samuel, where only the eight hundred thousand men are recorded, it does not say "all those of Israel," but merely "and Israel were," &c. It must also be borne in mind, that exclusively of the troops before mentioned, there was an army of observation on the frontiers of the Philistine's country composed of thirty thousand men, as appears by 2 Sam. 6: 1; and these it appears *were included* in the number of five hundred thousand of the people of Judah, which we find recorded in Samuel; but the author of

Chronicles, who mentions only four hundred and seventy thousand, gives the number of that tribe exclusively of those thirty thousand men, because they were not all of the tribe of Judah. And therefore he does not say " all those of Judah," as he had said " all those of Israel ;" but he only says, " and those of Judah." Here both accounts are fully explained and harmonized, merely by referring to other portions of Scripture treating on the same subject. Truly

" God is His own interpreter,
And He will make it plain."

103. David sinned in numbering the People.—And David's heart smote him after that he had numbered the people. And David said unto the Lord, *I have sinned* greatly in that I have done.—2 Sam, 24:10,

David NEVER sinned, EXCEPT IN THE MATTER OF URIAH.—David did that which was *right* in the eyes of the Lord, and turned not aside from anything that he commanded him all the days of his life, save only in the matter of Uriah the Hittite,—1 Kings 15: 5.

The one text in 2 Sam. 24: 10, presents David's confession of foolishness in the matter of numbering Israel. The Hebrew word here translated sinned is *gahtah,* and is defined by Gesenius thus: To miss, not to hit the mark, spoken of an archer, (see Judg. 20: 16,) also of the feet, to miss, to make a false step, to stumble and fall. To sin, to forfeit, to bear the loss of anything, &c., &c. See Gesenius, page 307.

Sin is a transgression of the law, and although it is evident that David did wrong, that he committed an error in his administration, as King of Israel, still in this act he violated no command or law of God, either written or oral, of which we have any account.

The other text teaches that David obeyed all the *commands* of God, except in the case of Uriah, the Hittite, and we challenge the skeptic to find *one* command or statute of God which David violated during his whole reign except this.

---

104.   One of the Penalties of David's sin was seven years *of famine.*—So Gad came to David and told him, Shall *seven* years of famine come unto thee in thy land ?—2 Sam. 24: 13.

*It was not seven, but **THREE** years of Famine.*—So Gad came to David and said unto him, Thus saith the Lord, choose thee either *three* years of famine,—1 Chr. 21: 11, 12.

In reference to this proposition we will merely remark upon the well known fact, that in Hebrew and Greek, numbers are expressed by the alphabetical characters. In Hebrew the letter *zain* signifies seven, while *gimel* denotes three, and the characters are so nearly alike that any translator might be excused for mistaking them, unless the type, ink, and paper, were of the *first quality*, which certainly was not the case at the time King James' version was given to the public.

In 2 Sam. 24: 13, the Septuagint reads, " shall *three* years of famine," &c., being the same as in Chronicles, and this is doubtless the true rendering.

---

105.   David took Seven Hundred Horsemen.—And David took from him a thousand chariots and seven *hundred* horsemen. 2 Sam. 8: 4.

*David took **SEVEN THOUSAND** Horsemen.*—And David took from him a thousand chariots and seven *thousand* horsemen.— 1 Chron. 18: 4.

60. A family, also as the subdivision of a tribe, Judg. 6: 15; 1 Sam. 10: 19, 1 Sam. 23: 23.— Spoken also of a city as the residence of such a family. Mic. 5: 1. See Gesenius' Hebrew Lexicon, page 59.

Hence we infer that while the number of horsemen captured is *explicitly* stated in 2 Sam. 8: 4, it is spoken of *indefinitely* in Chronicles; the word in this connection meaning simply a large or round number, and probably the word itself might, with equal propriety, be rendered, hundreds, thousands, or millions, but other portions of the divine Record state the matter so explicitly as to leave no possibility of being misunderstood.

106. David bought a Threshing Floor for fifty shekles of silver.—So David bought the threshing floor and the oxen for fifty shekles of silver.—2 Sam. 24: 24.

David bought the Threshing Foor for SIX HUNDRED shekles of gold.—So David gave to Ornan for the place six hundred shekles of gold.—1 Chr. 21 : 25.

We find by a careful examination of these two passages that the writer of the book of Samuel mentions only what David gave for the *threshing floor*, (a place only about six or eight yards wide) and the oxen and instruments of wood, (ver. 22) viz: fifty shekels of silver. But the writer of the book of Chronicles *does not* state the price David gave for these things, but informs us what he paid for *the whole place*, (ver. 25) that, is for the land upon which this threshing floor stood, viz: "six hundred shekels of gold, by weight." And history informs us that this "place" was actually that, which was afterwards called *Mount Zion*, being about nine hundred yards in length, and six hundred in width.

How easily every objection to God's word is removed by the clear light of honest investigation.

For eighteen hundred years this little volume has been exposed to the fire of the keenest criticism. Infidels of every age have sought to impeach its veracity, and question its authority. The mythology of the Illiad has passed away, the fables of the Shaster, the Talmud, and the Koran, have fallen before the lights of science and civilization. But the Bible lies before us to day unscathed, and untouched by man's puny efforts. It is still the glorious day-star of eternal truth, which guides the wandering feet of humanity through the wilderness of time, and leads them to the fair heights of the glory-clad mountains that arise beyond the tomb. It is the "Pillar Cloud," to the marching columns of God's little ones—guiding slowly, but guiding surely to the sun-lit plains of peace and gladness, that rest in the kingdom of God.

107. David's Throne was to endure forever.—Once have I sworn by my holiness that I will not lie unto David. His seed shall endure forever and his throne as the sun before me. It shall be established forever.—Ps. 89: 35, 36, 37.

David's throne was CAST DOWN.—Thou hast made his glory to cease and hast cast his throne down to the ground.—Ps. 89: 44.

Truly, "Thou hast made his glory to cease, and hast cast his throne down to the ground." But this statement, so far from being a *mistake* of the inspired penman, is confirmed by every Historical record, and not only so, but the fact here spoken of, is in itself a fulfillment of prophecy. For in reference to the last prince that reigned on David's throne, we read, "And thou profane wicked prince of Israel, whose day is come, when iniquity shall have an end. Thus saith the Lord God, remove the diadem, take off the crown, this shall not be the same ; exalt him that is low, and abase him that is high. I will overturn, overturn, overturn it, and it shall be no more, until *he* come whose *right it is* and I will give it him."—Ezek. 21: 25, 27.

Hence we learn that it was decreed in the counsels of eternal justice, that the kingdom of Israel should be overturned, and the crown removed and so it must remain—not *forever*, but until *he* comes whose *right it is* and God will give it him.

Was there ever a prediction more clearly fulfilled? Truly, the kingdom of Israel has been *overturned* by the Gentile nations of earth. The foot of the bloody Turk, the haughty Saracen, and the invincible Roman, have marred the glorious beauty of the land which was promised to Abraham, and given to Israel for an everlasting possession.

The diadem no longer gleams upon the brow of holy kings. The sons of Israel are scattered among the tribes of earth, and the Holy Land—the birth place of our Savior and Israel's sacred trust —that land which was hallowed above all others, has been made a bloody field of contest, where the armies of Europe have struggled for centuries. The temporal succession of her kings has ceased, Jerusalem has become heaps, and Zion a desolation. The "seven times" of Israel's captivity has hung its palling mantle over the throne and kingdom of David, and according to the declaration of Jehovah, they must remain in ruins, until *he* comes whose *right it is* and God will give it him. Hence, when the rightful heir appears, the throne will be restored and the kingdom reinstated. And the beautiful prophecy of Isaiah reveals the personage who is the legal heir of David's royal line. "For unto us a child is born, unto us a son is given, and the government shall be upon his shoulder, and his name shall be called Wonderful Counsellor, the Mighty God, the Everlasting Father, the Prince of Peace; of the increase of his government and peace there shall be no end, upon the throne of David and upon his kingdom, to order it and to establish it, with jus-. tice and with judgment, from henceforth even forever—the zeal of the Lord of Hosts shall perform this." See Isa. 9: 6, 7.

See also the Pentecostal sermon in Acts 2: 29, 34, which reads thus: "Men and brethren let me freely speak unto you of the patriarch David, that he is both dead and buried and his sepulchre is with us to this day. Therefore being a prophet and knowing that God had sworn with an oath *that of the fruit of his loins, according to the flesh he would raise up Christ to sit on his throne."—* And in the promise of the angel to Mary, we find the words, "He shall be great, and shall be called the son of the Highest, *and the Lord God shall give unto him the throne of his father David and he shall reign over the house of Jacob forever, and of his kingdom there shall be no end."* See also 1 Chron. 7: 11, 22 ; 2 Sam. 7: 8, 26 ; Zech. 6: 12, 13 ; Jer. 21: 27, 34 ; Ezek. 37: 15, 28 ; Hos. 3: 4, 5. Read also, in connection with the above, the 4th chapter of Isaiah, and Hebrew 1: 8.

Hence, *Jesus of Nazareth,* the Messiah of the Hebrew Scriptures, and the *Christos* of the Greek, is the only legal heir of David's throne, and he has never yet been seated there. He is now upon the *throne of God* at the Father's right hand, expecting till his enemies are made his footstool. See Heb. 12: 1, 2. Heb. 8: 1. Heb. 10: 12, 14.

A Spiritual throne erected in the Heavens could not fill the promise, for David never reigned there ; no throne in Heaven was ever overturned or destroyed, and therefore can never be restored. "Behold the days come saith the Lord, that I will raise unto David a righteous branch, and a king shall reign and prosper, and shall execute judgment and justice in the land. In his days Judah shall be saved, and Israel shall dwell safely, and this is the name whereby he shall be called, *the Lord our Righteousness.*" Jer. 23: 5–8.— Please see Psalm 89: 3, 4. Amos 9: 11. Ezek. 47: 1, 12. Ps. 22: 28.

Therefore, when Jesus returns from the Heavens, and the long promised *Millennium* dawns upon earth—when Israel is brought back from Gentile bondage and inherits the promised land—when Judah and Israel are no more two nations, and one king shall be king to them all—when the glory of the Lord shall be revealed, and all flesh shall see it together—when the kingdom is the Lord's, and he is the governor among the nations—when His glory shall cover the earth, as the waters cover the deep—then indeed will the tabernacle of God be with men, and the oath of Jehovah to David will be accomplished.

Our space forbids anything but the briefest possible sketch of this glorious theme. We can only cite a *few* texts out of the *multitude* that sustain our position; but we trust that enough has already been said, to convince even the mind of a skeptic, of the beautiful harmony and perfect consistency of those passages of Holy Writ, which he has heretofore supposed to be at variance with each other.

We now come to the department of our work which the infidel is pleased to term " Speculative Doctrines," but if he had spent the same amount of time in *studying* the Scriptures, that he has employed in unfair compilation—if he were learned in the wisdom of God, he would know there was nothing "speculative" in the glorious truths which Jehovah has revealed to man.

108. Christ is Equal with God.—I and my Father are one.— John 10: 30. Who, being in the form of God, thought it not robbery to be *equal* with God.—Phil. 2: 5.

Christ is NOT Equal with God.—My Father is *greater* than I.— John 14: 28. Of that day and hour knoweth no man, no, not the angels of heaven, but my Father only.—Matt. 24: 36.

John 10: 30, is beautifully explained by the connection; please read what Christ says in speaking of his disciples, verse 29. "My Father which gave them unto me, is greater than all; and no man is able to pluck them out of my Father's hand. I and my Father are one." (Greek, one thing.) "To snatch my true disciples out of my hand, would be to snatch them out of my Father's hand, because I and my Father are one— one in design, action, agreement and affection." See Newcomb. Christ also prays for his disciples to become *one*, in the same sense that he and the Father are one. See John 17: 11, 21, 22.— And certainly he never intended to pray that they might all become one person. See also Gal. 3: 28.

In Phil. 2: 5, we read, " Who being in the form of God, thought it not robbery to be equal with God," that is, he did not regard it as an act of injustice to the Father, for him to exert on proper occasions, his miraculous powers. But King James' version is a little ambiguous here. McKnight renders the verse thus, " Who being in the form of God, did not think it robbery to be *like* God." Wakefield translates the text as follows : " Who though in a divine form, did not think of eagerly retaining this Divine likeness, but emptied (or divested) himself of it, by taking a servant's form ; and being like other men with the dispositions of a man, he became so obedient as to humble himself unto death, even death upon a cross." It must be borne in mind that the previous verses are an exhortation to humility, and the lowly Jesus is here mentioned, as an example to believers. See also the Diaglott, and Newcomb's Improved Version, on this point. It is the *uniform* teaching of the New Testament, that the Father is greater than the Son.

**109. *Jesus was All Powerful.*—*All* power is given unto me in heaven and in earth.—Matt. 28: 18. The Father loveth the Son and hath given *all* things into his hand.—John 3: 35.

Jesus was NOT All Powerful.—And he could there do no mighty work, save that he laid his hands on a few sick folks and healed them.—Mark 6: 5.

The " all power," spoken of in Matt. 28: 18, was the Gospel and miraculous power delegated to him by his Father. Mark 6: 5, the Diaglott gives as follows : " And he was *unwilling* to do any miracles there, except a few sick persons he cured by laying his hands on them." See Matt. 13: 58 ; Mark 9: 23

**110. *The Law was Superceded by the Christian Dispensation.*—The law and the prophets were *until* John ; since that time the kingdom of God is preached.—Luke 16: 16. Having *abolished* in the flesh the enmity, even the *law* of commandments contained in ordinances.—Eph. 2: 15. But now we are *delivered* from the law — Rom. 7: 6.

The Law was NOT Superceded by the Christian Dispensation.—I am come *not* to destroy the *law* but to fulfill. For verily I say unto you, till heaven and earth shall pass, one jot or tittle shall *in no wise pass from the law* till all be fulfilled. Whosoever therefore shall break one of the least commandments and shall teach men so, he shall be called the least in the kingdom of heaven.— Matt. 5: 17, 18, 19.

Verily, Christ came not to destroy the law—he did not come to violate the obligation men are under, to have their lives regulated by moral precepts, or to dissolve the reference it has to things promised. But he says, " I am come to *complete* (*pleroosai*) or *perfect* and *accomplish* every thing shadowed forth in the Mosaic ritual, to *fill up* its great design, and to teach my followers to fill up or complete every moral duty. Christ *completed* the law, which was in itself, only the shadow or typical representation of things to come. He added to it that which was necessary to make it perfect, viz: *the sacrifice of himself*, without which it could neither satisfy God, nor benefit man ; for it is to " the *Lamb* slain from the foundation of the world," that its types and shadows refer. One jot nor one tittle would not pass from the law until all be fulfilled ; one jot or one *yod* is the smallest letter in the Hebrew alphabet, and one tittle or *point* probably means those *points* which served for vowels in the language, if they then existed—if not, they must refer to the *apices* or points of certain letters, such as *resh, daleth, he* or *cheth*. The change of any of these into the other, would make a most essential alteration in the sense, or as the Rabbins say, " destroy the world." Hence the above expression of Jesus is full of emphasis, and though all the forces of the universe should join together to prevent the accomplishment of the great designs of the Most High, it is all in vain—not even the sense of a single letter shall be lost, for the *words* of Jehovah are unchangeable and immutable.

"Wherefore the law was our schoolmaster to bring us unto Christ." Gal. 3: 24. Christ came not to *destroy* the law, but to *fulfill* it, and being *fulfilled*, its work is done. "For Christ is the *end of the law* for righteousness to every one that believeth." Rom. 10: 4. So that "Now we are delivered from the law," and the texts quoted in the first part of the above proposition are not only in perfect harmony with Matt. 5: 17, 18, 19, but are the statements whereby it is confirmed.

111. Christ's Mission was Peace.—And suddenly there was with the angels a multitude of the heavenly hosts praising God and saying, Glory to God in the highest, and on earth *peace.*—Luke 2: 13, 14.

Christ's Mission was NOT Peace.—Think not that I am come to send peace on earth; I came *not* to send peace, but a sword.—Matt 10: 34.

At the time of the birth of our Savior, a choir of angels chanted the words, " Glory to God in the highest, and on earth peace and good will to men." But the Savior himself says, "Think not that I am come to send peace on earth—I came not to send peace, but a sword." Still by referring to God's word as a *unit*, the great umpire of our investigations, the harmony and consistency of its teachings are apparent. John 16: 33, explains both passages. "These things have I spoken unto you, that in *me* ye might have peace; in the *world* ye have tribulation." No language could make our proposition plainer. While the legitimate effects of Christ's precepts, when believed and obeyed, are *peace* to the willing and obedient, the natural enmity between good and evil can never be subdued, until wrong ceases to exist. "Therefore, being justified by faith, we have peace with God, through our Lord Jesus Christ." Rom. 5: 1 Christ came to bring "the *peace* of God *which passeth all understanding*," to all who would believe and obey the " *Gospel of peace*," but he will surely send a sword upon the enemies of God and the foes of his people.

"I create the fruit of the lips. Peace, peace to him that is far off, and to him that is near, saith the Lord; and I will heal him. But the wicked are like the troubled sea, when it cannot rest, whose waters cast up mire and dirt. There is no *peace*, saith my God, to the *wicked*." Isa. 57: 19, 20, 21 ; Isa. 48: 22.

112. *Christ Received not testimony from Man.*—Ye sent unto John and he bear witness unto the truth. But I receive *not* testimony from man.—John 5: 33, 34.

Christ DID Receive Testimony from Man.—And ye also shall bear witness, because ye have been with me from the beginning. John 15: 16.

The witness spoken of in John 15: 27, was that which his disciples bore *to others*, for they had no need to testify to Jesus, neither was it necessary for him to require (see Wakefield,) testimony from man, for he had the testimony of *God himself*. He says, " But I have *greater witness* than that of John; for the works which the Father hath given me to finish, the same works that I do, bear witness of me that the Father hath sent me. And the Father himself which sent me hath borne witness of me " See John 5: 36, 37.

113. *Christ's Witness of Himself is True.*—I am one that bear witness of myself.........Though I bear record of myself, yet *my record is true*.—John 8: 18, 14.

Christ's Witness of Himself is NOT True.—If I bear witness of myself, *my witness is not true*.—John 5: 31.

Bishop Pearce, Wakefield, and the Diaglott, translate John 5: 31, *interrogatively ;* they read, "If I bear witness of myself, is not my *witness true ?"* This version (which is sustained by the Greek, rather than the other,) obviates all difficulty. His own testimony that he was the Messiah, was *perfectly true,* and might have been sufficient for condemning a world of unbelievers; but he also had the testimony of John, which he did not need, although he was an unimpeachable witness; he also had the testimony of his disciples, and multitudes of others who had witnessed his miracles, but all human testimony was superfluous, for he had the witness of *Jehovah himself* See John 5: 36, 37; 1 John 5: 9; John 3: 2· John 10: 25; John 15: 24; Matt. 3: 17; Matt. 17: 5.

114. Christ laid down his Life for his Friends.—Greater love hath no man than this, that a man *lay down* his life for his friends.—John 15: 13. The good shepherd giveth his life for the sheep, John 10: 11.

Christ laid down his Life for his ENEMIES.—When we were enemies, we were reconciled to God by the death of his Son.—Rom. 5: 10.

During the life time of the Son of God, he made the following forcible remark: "Greater love hath no man than this, that a man lay down his life for his friends." How true! No man can carry his love for his friend farther than this, for when he gives up his life, he gives up all he has. And it is only in the *rarest instances* that *such* friendship has been known in earth's history. But when Jehovah's Son "poured out his soul unto death," he laid down his life, not only for his friends, but he also *died for his enemies,* thereby giving the universe an example of love to the world, which was without precedent in the annals of mankind.

115. *It was Lawful for the Jews to put Christ to Death.*—The Jews answered him, We have a law, and by our law he *ought* to die.—John 19: 7.

It was NOT Lawful for the Jews to put Him to Death.—The Jews therefore said unto him, It is *not lawful* for us to put any man to death.—John 18: 31.

In Lev. 24: 14-16, we find that blasphemers of God were to be put to death; and the chief priests, having charged Jesus with blasphemy, voted that he deserved to die. But it must be remembered that the Jews were at this time subject to the Romans, and consequently they could not be allowed to administer capital punishment to criminals. Hence, although they might have judged Jesus according to their own law, (as Pilate bade them,) they could only excommunicate or scourge him.

The power of life and death was in all probability taken from the Jews when Archelaus, king of Judea, was banished to Vienna, and Judea was made a Roman province; and this happened more than fifty years before the destruction of Jerusalem. But the Romans suffered Herod—mentioned in Acts 12—to exercise the power of life and death during his reign. See Calmet and Pearce.

116. *Children are Punished for the Sins of their Parents.*—I am a jealous God, visiting the iniquities of the fathers upon the children.—Ex. 20: 5.

Children are NOT Punished for the Sins of their Parents. The son shall *not* bear the iniquities of the father.—Ezek. 18; 20.

Ex. 20: 5, is a declaration which accompanies the second commandment, in the decalogue given to Israel.

Idolatry is the sin which God is denouncing. And after they had broken his law by worshiping idols, the Divine protection was withdrawn, and the Israelites were delivered up into the hands of their enemies, for the gods in which they had trusted could not deliver them; and they remained in bondage, and their children after them, to the third and fourth generations successively, as confirmed by every part of Jewish history. And this became the grand, effectual and lasting means, in the hand of God for their final deliverance from idolatry; for after the Babylonish captivity, the Israelites never disgraced themselves with idolatry, as they had formerly done. Hence it appears that *national* judgments, which pass from generation to generation, are those referred to in the text above.— Perhaps it also refers to *natural laws* by the violation of which one man or woman may impart disease to several successive generations. And in relation to financial affairs, children often lose their patrimony, and suffer with poverty in consequence of the extravigance and folly of their parents. And in political crimes, the blood of nobility is tainted by the rebellion of an ancestor, and the children can only be restored to their rightful position by an act of royal favor. But this law only refers to the temporal existence, and has no bearing upon the reward or punishment which is to be bestowed at the resurrection. This point is beautifully exemplified in the eighteenth chapter of Ezekiel. Please read as follows, commencing at the fourth verse :

" Behold all souls are mine ; as the soul of the father so also the soul of the son is mine ; the soul that sinneth it shall die, (*i. e.* the second death, which is the doom pronounced upon the ungodly.) But if a man be just, and do that which is lawful and right.. . Hath walked in my statutes, and hath kept my judgments; to deal truly, he is just, *he shall surely live*, (shall have the eternal life, which is promised to the righteous.) But if *he* beget a son that is a robber, a shedder of blood, &c., he *shall surely die*, (the second death).— Now lo, if *he* beget a son that seeketh all the father's sins, which he hath done, and considereth and doeth not such....*he shall surely live.* 20 verse, "The son shall not bear the iniquity of the father, (in the future state,) neither shall the father bear the iniquity of the son, the righteousness of the righteous, shall be upon him, and the wickedness of the wicked shall be upon *him*."

It is probable the first verse of the chapter is designed to correct a wrong impression, in reference to the law, which was prevalent among the Jews, and not to convey the idea that the law itself was repealed.

117. Man is Justified by Faith Alone.—By the deeds of the law there shall no flesh be justified.—Rom. 3: 20. Knowing that a man is not justified by the works of the law, but by the faith of Jesus Christ.—Gal. 2: 16. The just shall live by faith. And the law is not of faith.—Gal. 3: 11, 12. For if Abraham were justified by works he hath whereof to glory.—Rom. 4: 2.

Man is NOT Justified by Faith Alone.—Was not Abraham our father justified by works?.........Ye see then how that by works a man is justified, and *not by faith* only.—Jam. 2: 21, 24. The doers of the law shall be justified.—Rom. 2: 13.

The only texts in the above proposition, which seem to require any notice at our hands, are the two last quoted, and they are beautifully explained by the context. Please read James 2: 20-24. But wilt thou know, O, vain man, that faith without works is dead ? Was not Abraham, our father, justified by works, when he had *offered* Isaac, his son, upon the altar ? *Seest thou, how faith wrought with his works, and by works was faith made perfect ?*

And the Scripture was fulfilled which saith, Abraham believed God, and it was imputed unto him for righteousness, and he was called the

Friend of God. Ye see, then, how that by works, a man is justified and not by faith only.— We see, then, that Abraham's justification was dependent upon *faith and works both.* See also Romans 2: 12-13. For as many as have sinned without law, shall also perish without law, and as many as have sinned in the law, shall be judged by the law. (For not the hearers of the law are just before God, but the doers of the law shall be justified, &c.) The last verse is par- enthetical, and refers of course to those, and those alone, who were under the law. It is thrown in to explain the preceding verse, and conveys the idea that it was not necessary alone to be hear- ers of the law, but they must also have been doers of it, in order to be justified, when the great day of reward comes to the inhabitants of earth. When the judge of the quick and dead shall bestow the honors of eternity, those who lived under the law, and were faithful to its requirements, shall receive a just recompense of reward.

118. It is Impossible to Fall from Grace.—And I give unto them eternal life, and they shall *never perish,* neither shall any pluck them out of my hand.—John 10: 25. Neither death, nor life, nor angels, nor principalities, nor powers, nor things present, nor things to come, nor height nor depth, nor any other creature, shall be able to separate us from the love of God which is in Christ our Lord.— Rom. 8: 38, 39.

It IS Possible to Fall from Grace.—But when the righteous man *turneth away* from his righteousness, and committeth iniquity, and doeth according to all the abominations that the wicked man doeth, shall he live? All his righteousness that he hath done shall not be mentioned; in his trespass that he hath trespassed, and in his sin that he hath sinned, in them shall he die.—Ezek. 18: 24. For it is impossible for those who were once enlightened, and have tasted of the heavenly gift, and are made partakers of the Holy Ghost, and have tasted the good word of God, and the powers of the world to come, if they *shall fall away,* to renew them again unto repen- tance,—Heb. 6: 4-6. For if, after they have escaped the pollu- tions of the world through the knowledge of the Lord and Savior

Jesus Christ, they are again entangled therein and overcome, the latter end is worse than the beginning. For it had been better for them not to have known the way of righteousness, than after they had known it, to *turn from* the holy commandment delivered unto them.—2 Pet. 2: 20, 21.

John 10: 28 explains itself so clearly that it hardly needs a comment. He says, "I give unto them eternal life, and (then) they shall never perish, neither shall any pluck them out of my hand." Of course, the promise that they shall never perish is contingent upon their reception of "the gift of God, which is eternal life through Jesus Christ our Lord."—Rom. 6: 23.— They must receive the eternal life promised to the righteous before they become imperishable, and *that* they cannot obtain until the coming age of glory, when God shall be all in all. See Mark 10: 30.

Eternal life is promised as a reward to those who by patient continuance in well doing seek for glory honor and immortality.—Rom. 2: 7.— And the promise standeth *sure*, for "Behold the Lord will come with strong hand, and his arm shall rule for him; behold his *reward is with him*, and his work before him."

And so long as we remain faithful to the commands of God, so long as we abide in him, and he in us, "Neither death, nor life, nor angels, nor principalities, nor powers, nor things present, nor things to come, nor height, nor depth, nor any other creature, shall be able to separate us from the love of God, which is in Christ our Lord." But if "after they have escaped the pollutions of the world, through the knowledge of the Lord and Savior, Jesus Christ, they are again entangled therein, and overcome, the latter end is worse than the beginning. For it had been better for them *not to have known* the way of righteousness, than after they had known it to turn from the holy cammandment delivered unto them." Hence, it is clear that nothing but *our own unfaithfulness* can separate us from the love of God.

119. No Man is Without Sin.—For there is *no* man that sinneth not.—1 Kings 8: 46. Who can say, I have made my heart clean; I am pure from my sin?—Prov. 20: 9. For there is *not a just man* upon the earth, that doeth good and sinneth not.—Eccl. 7: 20. There is *none* righteous, no, *not one.*—Rom. 3: 10.

Christians are SINLESS.—Whosoever is born of God doth *not* commit sin.........he *cannot sin*, because he is born of God.........Whosoever abideth in him sinneth not. He that committeth sin is of the devil.—1 John 3: 9, 6, 8.

It is certainly true, as indicated by the first class of texts here quoted, that perfection doth not dwell with the children of men—that man, however pure and upright his motives and intentions may be, is liable to err from the path of rectitude, and fail in the performance of duty.— But it is equally true, that " Whosoever is born of God doth not commit sin.... he cannot sin, because he is born of God."

But we cannot be born of God until we are changed, when this mortal shall put on immortality, and this corruptible shall put on incorruptability, then indeed shall we be born of God.— See John 3: 5-8. And having lost the sinful nature, which Adam transmitted to his posterity, we shall be free from the possibility of sinning.— " Whosoever committeth sin is of the devil."— The Diaglott renders this text as follows, " He who *practices* sin is of the enemy." The idea is, that he who practices sin—sins willfully and persistently, is of the devil. " Whosoever abideth in him, sinneth not ;" that is, he is not a constitutional sinner, he does not sin willfully, or persistently. " If we sin or err we have an advocate with the Father, even Jesus Christ the righteous." There is a great difference between the errors and frailties, which are inseparable from our fallen nature, and that willful and determinate or reckless course, which is pursued by many, in direct opposition to the known will and law of Jehovah.

It must be borne in mind, in cases like the above, that one word frequently has several legitimate definitions, which may vary considerably from each other. Language is composed of words, and words are the mere representation of ideas. In proportion to the poverty of a language, that is, in porportion to the fewness of its words, must each word have a variety of meanings. That this was particularly the case with the ancient languages, every one must know who stops to consider that each word, (even in the English tongue, which is so *rich*,) has a variety of significations. For instance, the word "flesh" signifies a part of the physical organization, or human nature, or carnality, or corrupt nature, or the present life, or legal righteousness, or tenderness, human feeling, kindred, stock, family, or the soft pulpy substance of fruit, &c.— And the word "give" signifies to bestow, to impart, to communicate, to pay, to yield, to lend, to quit, to grant, to expose, to yield to the power of, to empower, to produce, &c. See Webster.— And the word "sin" also has a variety of meanings, especially in the original. But when an infidel meets with any of these, or other words of the same class in the Bible, although they may have a dozen other significations, he invariably annexes to them that meaning, and that only, (provided they have one that *can* be thus construed,) which will tend to impeach the holiness, the justice or veracity of Jehovah. To such lengths of injustice and dishonesty are they driven, to support their awful rebellion against the authority of the Most High.

120. There is to be a Resurrection of the Dead.—The trumpet shall sound and the dead shall be raised.—1 Cor. 15: 52. And I saw the dead, small and great, stand before God.........and they were judged, every man according to their works.—Rev. 20: 12, 13. Now that the dead are raised even Moses showed at the bush, when he called the Lord the God of Abraham, and the God of Isaac, and the God of Jacob.—Luke 20: 37. For if the dead rise not, then is not Christ raised.—1 Cor. 15, 16.

There is to be NO Resurrection of the Dead;—As the cloud is consumed and vanisheth away, so he that goeth down to the grave shall come up no more.—Job 7: 9. The dead know not anything, neither have they any more a reward.—Eccl. 29: 14. They are dead, *they shall not live;* they are deceased, they *shall not rise.*—Is. 25: 14.

The word of God is *uniform* in its teaching, that "The trumpet shall sound and the dead shall be raised." "For if the dead rise not, then is Christ not raised." In reference to Job 7: it will be seen by carefully reading the connection, that the *whole chapter* is one of Job's laments during his sore affliction, and pertains *only* to the present life, the future state is not alluded to at all. It is merely the mournful boundaries of the natural life, as they appeared to Job in his deep trial.— The 9th verse reads, "As the cloud is consumed and vanisheth away, so he that goeth down to the grave shall come up no more;" and if the resurrection were the subject under discussion, and if this text were placed in the inspired volume without explanation, then indeed should we be left upon the ocean of time with *no hope,* and the cold starless night of oblivion would settle down upon the graves of those we love. But the next verse clearly explains the meaning of the author. It reads, "He shall return no more *to his house,* neither shall his place know him any more." And hence we have found the solution of the whole matter; the dead cannot return and mingle with the living, upon the shores of time, for they *sleep in the dust.* Truly, the author of the book of Job was far from being a Spiritualist!

Eccl. 9: 5, simply teaches that death is a sleep, that the inhabitants of the grave "*know not anything*," until they are awakened out of their slumber and aroused to consciousness, by the trump of the Archangel. Please see Job 14: 21. Job 10: 13. Isa. 63: 16. Ps. 6: 5. Ps. 88: 10–12. Ps. 15: 17. Acts 2: 29, 34. Isa. 38: 18, 19. Dan. 12: 2. Acts 7: 60. Luke 20: 35. Acts 24: 21. Acts 26: 6–8. 1 Cor. 15: 17–19. Ps. 146: 4. John 5: 28–29. 1 Thess. 4: 13, 17. In relation to the clause, "neither have they any more a reward," it is only necessary to direct attention to the *tense* of the verb. The text does not say that they shall never have a reward, but simply that they *do not* have it while in the cold embrace of death; hence the declaration is in perfect harmony with every text in the inspired volume bearing upon this theme. For there is no reward promised the children of God, until the Apocalypse of his Son from Heaven. See Matt. 16: 27, and Rev. 22: 12.

The class spoken of in Isaiah 26: 14, is the class of tyrants of whom it is expressly said that God *had visited and destroyed them*, and having received from the hand of Jehovah, the punishment which their crimes merited, it is by no means essential to the harmony of the Scriptures, that they should be raised in the general resurrection. If God has destroyed them by a *special judgment*, he can certainly decree that *they* shall not come again from the dead, without conflicting with his plan concerning humanity as a race

121. *Reward and Punishment to be Bestowed in this World.* —Behold the righteous shall be recompensed in the *earth*, much more the wicked and the sinner.—Prov. 11: 31.

Reward and Punishment to be Bestowed in the NEXT World. —And the dead were judged out of those things which were written in the books, according to their works,—Rev. 20: 12. Then he shall reward every man according to his works.—Matt. 16: 27. According to that he hath done, whether it be good or bad.—2 Cor. 5: 10.

How true the statement, that " The righteous shall be recompensed in the earth, much more the wicked and the sinner." And the skeptic has not, nor *can not* quote a *single text*, which does not *perfectly* harmonize with the above. The other three texts cited in his proposition, bear upon the *time* of the judgment and reward, but they say nothing about the *locality*. The *uniform* teaching of God's word, upon this point is, that the reward of the righteous and the punishment of the wicked, are alike to be bestowed upon this planet See Matt. 5: 5. Rev. 5: 10. Dan. 7: 27. Ps. 37: 9, 10, 11, 22, 29. Isa. 60: 21. Prov. 2: 22. Dan. 2: 44. Luke 1: 33

122. *Annihilation the Portion of all Mankind.*—Why died not I from the womb? Why did I not give up the ghost when I came out of the belly ?.........For now should I have lain still and been quiet; I should have slept : then had I been at rest, with kings and counsellors of the earth, which built desolate places for themselves; or with princes that had gold, who filled their houses with silver ; or as a hidden, untimely birth I had not been ; as infants which never saw the light. There the wicked cease from troubling, and there the weary be at rest.........The small and great are there, and the servant is free from his master. Wherefore is light given to him that is in misery, and life unto the bitter in soul, which long for death and it cometh not.........which rejoice exceedingly when they have found the grave?—Job 3: 11, 13-17, 19-22. The *dead know not anything*.........For there is no work, nor device, nor knowledge, nor wisdom in the grave whither thou goest.—Eccl. 9: 5, 10.— For that which befalleth the sons of men befalleth the beasts, even one thing befalleth them: as the one dieth, so dieth the other ; yea, they have all one breath ; so that a man hath no preeminence above a beast.........All go unto one place. Eccl. 3: 19, 20.

ENDLESS MISERY the Portion of a PART of Mankind. —These shall go away into *everlasting punishment,*—Matt. 25: 46.— And the devil that deceived them was cast into the lake of fire and brimstone, where the beast and the false prophet are, and shall be *tormented day and night for ever and ever*.........And whosoever was not found written in the book of life was cast into the lake of fire.— Rev. 20: 10, 15. And the smoke of their *torment* ascendeth up forever and ever.—Rev. 14: 11. And many of them that sleep in the dust shall awake, some to everlasting life, and some to shame and everlasting contempt.—Dan. 12: 2.

The first class of texts here quoted, refer to the
state of the dead, between death and the resurrection; and the second, although they refer to the
destiny of the wicked, must be grossly perverted,
in order to sustain the infidel's proposition that
" *endless misery* is the portion of a part of mankind." True, " These shall go away into everlasting punishment," but it does not say everlasting *torture*, and the punishment here alluded to is
defined in 2 Thess. 1: 9, to be everlasting *destruction.*

The next text under consideration, is Rev. 20:
10, 15, and says nothing about anybody, except
the *devil*, the *beast* and the *false prophet*, and
hence has no bearing upon the destiny of mankind. It may be well however to remark, that the
Greek phrase in the above text, which is rendered
"for ever and ever," is " *eis aioonas toon aioonoon*"
and signifies literally, "until the age of ages,"
hence it will be seen that even the punishment
here alluded to, is *limited* in its duration.

And in relation to Rev. 14: 11, it will be seen
by the connection that it only refers to that special
class of sinners who have been guilty of " worshiping the *beast* and his *image*," and the original
reads here precisely as in the preceding text, and
it should be rendered thus: And the smoke of
their torment ascendeth up until the age of ages,
hence the suffering is here also *limited.*

So far as Dan. 12: 2, is concerned, we cannot
see as it bears upon the skeptics proposition at all,
for no one will for a moment contend that it is necessary for any one to *live* forever, in order to be
the subject of " *everlasting contempt.*" The records of History present many ignominious characters for the everlasting contempt of posterity, who
have slumbered in the dust for ages. A God of
mercy has *never* threatened frail humanity with
an eternity of torture; his Word is a *unit* on this

theme, as well as all others, and it declares that the. wicked *shall not* live forever. See John 3: 36. 1 John 3: 15. 1 John 5: 11, 12. John 6: 53. Deut. 30: 19, 20.

The declaration of Jehovah is, that *they shall die.* See Ezek. 18: 4, 20, 24, 26, 31, 32.— Rom. 5: 21, 23. Rom. 7: 5. James 1: 15.— Rom. 6: 16. Rom. 8: 13. Rev. 21: 8. James 5: 19, 20.

The Bible says the wicked *shall perish.* Please read Job 20: 4, 7. Ps. 92: 9. Rom. 2: 12. Ps. 49: 20. Ps. 73: 27. Prov. 19: 9. Ps. 37: 20.— John 3: 14, 17. Luke 13: 2, 5. Ps. 2: 10, 12. 2 Pet. 2: 12.

God's word declarés *they shall be cut off.* Ps. 55: 4, 5. Ps. 37: 9, 22, 28, 34, 38. Ps. 94: 23.— Nah. 1: 15. Prov. 2: 21, 22.

The declaration of Jehovah is, that *they shall be destroyed.* Job 21: 23, 29, 30. Ps. 145: 20. Rom. 9: 22. Ps. 55: 23. Ps. 5: 6. Prov. 16: 18. Prov. 13: 13. Isa 1: 28. Prov; 13: 20. Phil. 3: 18, 19. Rom. 3: 15, 17. 2 Pet. 3: 16. Prov. 29: 1. Matt. 7: 13. Matt. 10: 28. Acts 3: 21. 2 Pet. 2: 12. Ps. 112: 7. Ps. 37: 38. Ps. 73: 3, 17, 18. 2 Thess. 1: 9, 10. Rev. 11: 18. 1 Thess. 5: 3.

The Bible says the wicked *shall be consumed.* Zeph. 1: 1, 2. Ps. 37: 20. Isa. 1: 28. Ps. 59: 13. Ps. 104; 35.

God's word distinctly states that they shall be *burned up root and branch.* Please read Matt. 13: 30.— Matt. 3: 12. John 15: 6. Ps. 117: 3. Isa. 1: 81. Isa. 33: 14. Heb. 6: 7, 8. Mal. 4: 13.

And they shall be as though they had not been.— See Ps. 58: 7, 11. Isa. 29: 20. Isa. 40: 12. Ps. 37: 10. Obed. 15, 16.

123. The Earth is to be Destroyed.—The earth also and the works that are therein shall be *burned up.*—2 Pet. 3: 10. They shall *perish,* but thou remainest.—Heb. 1: 11, And I saw a great white throne, and him that sat on it, from whose face the *earth* and the

heaven *fled away*, and there was no place found for them.—Rev.
20: 11.

The Earth is NEVER to be Destroyed.—Who laid the foundations of the earth that it should not be removed forever.—Ps. 104: 5
But the *earth abideth forever.*—Prov. 1: 4.

That the earth is to endure forever, and unfold
in its future history the glory of God, no one who
has studied the word of inspiration upon this subject will deny. The infidel however, finds what
appears to him a contradiction, of this plain doctrine of revelation, in 2 Pet. 3: 10. Heb. 1: 11.
Rev. 20: 11. But we shall endeavor to show that
the apparent discrepancy, is caused by the mist in
the brains of the compiler.

In reference to 2 Peter 3: 10, it does not require a very critical examination of the passage
to ascertain its meaning. Please read the whole
verse. "But the day of the Lord will come as a
thief in the night; in which the heavens shall
pass away with a great noise, and the elements
shall *melt with fervent heat*, and the *earth also ;*
and the *works* that are therein shall be burned
up." This is the obvious meaning of the text,
and the skeptic will please remember that *punctua-
tion* is not *inspiration*, and therefore the Bible is
by no means responsible for the manner in which
man has punctuated it.

The term "heavens and earth," is frequently
used in the Scriptures to denote *dispensations*, and
there are *three* alluded to in the Bible. The
heavens and earth that existed before the flood,
the heavens and earth that exist at present, and
the new heavens and new earth which the Apostle looked for. Peter says, in speaking of the
flood, "By the word of God the heavens were of
old, and the earth standing out of the water and
in the water, whereby the world that then was
perished. But no one will contend that the physical earth perished; the same hills and valleys

now smile with verdure that were then swept by the restless waves of the flood. It was the outward order and constitution of things which existed in antediluvian times, that were obliterated. And the fact that "we look for a new heavens and new earth wherein dwelleth righteousness," by no means indicates the destruction of the physical earth, but merely that the order of things shall be changed—the heavens and the earth shall be *renewed* by the mandate of Jehovah. The earth shall not pass away, it shall live on—survive its baptism of fire, and exist through its regeneration, and when the curse is removed, it shall smile in more than Eden gladness, while the endless ages of eternity circle around the throne of Jehovah, Ps. 119: 90. Eccl. 1: 4. Ps. 104: 5.

Time and space forbid a critical examination of this interesting theme, but we will remark, that in those passages which speak of the "end of the world," the word rendered *world*, is either *aioon*, which signifies a space of time, an age, an era, or a dispensation; or it is *kosmos*, which denotes the exterior order, arrangements, and political constitution of the earth, and these shall surely terminate when Christ comes, and give place to the new dispensation of peace and glory which is to dawn upon earth at his advent.

124. *No Evil shall Happen to the Godly.*—There shall *no evil* happen to the just.—Prov. 12: 21. Who is he that will harm you if ye be followers of that which is good.—1 Pet. 3: 13

Evil DOES Happen to the Godly.—Whom the Lord loveth he chasteneth, and scourgeth every son whom he receiveth.—Heb. 12: 6. And the Lord said unto Satan, Hast thou considered my servant Job, that there is none like him, a perfect and upright man ?........., So went Satan forth........, and smote Job with sore boils from the sole of his foot unto the crown of his head,—Job 2: 3. 7.

We fail to see any want of harmony here.— God has promised that no evil should come upon the just, which is true; but He has seen it to be for his own glory, and the good of man, to chastise his children—not indeed to inflict evil, but as an actual benefit. Heb. 12: 11, "Now no chastening for the present seemeth to be joyous, but grievous: nevertheless, afterward it yieldeth the peaceable fruit of righteousness unto them which are exercised thereby." An earthly parent does not punish his child for the purpose of injuring it, but that it may be thereby benefited. How then should we look upon the chastisement of him who pitieth those who fear him, even as a tender father his children? Hence the difficulty at once vanishes, and we only wonder that it should have been named as an objection.

125. *Worldly Good and Prosperity the Lot of the Godly.*— There shall no evil happen to the just.—Prov. 12: 21. For the Lord loveth judgment and forsaketh not his saints; they are preserved forever.........The wicked watcheth for the righteous and seeketh to slay him. The Lord will not leave him in his hand, nor condemn him when he is judged.........Mark the perfect man, and behold the upright; for the end of that man is peace.—Ps. 37: 28, 32, 33, 37.— Blessed is the man that walketh not in the counsel of the ungodly. Whatsoever he doeth shall prosper.—Ps. 1: 1, 3. And the Lord was with Joseph, and he was a *prosperous* man.—Gen. 39: 2. So the Lord blessed the latter end of Job more than the beginning,—Job 42: 12.

Worldly MISERY and DESTITUTION the Lot of the Godly. —They were stoned, they were sawn asunder, they were tempted; were slain with the sword; they wandered about in sheep-skins and goat-skins: being destitute, afflicted, tormented.........they wandered in deserts, and in mountains, and in dens and caves of the earth.—Heb. 11: 37, 38. These are they which came out of *great tribulation.*—Rev. 7: 14. Yea, and all that will live godly in Christ Jesus shall suffer persecution.—2 Tim. 3: 12. And ye shall be *hated of all men* for my name's sake.—Luke 21: 17.

This proposition is so similar to the preceeding one that it hardly needs a reply at our hands.— We may however, remark that the persecutions which fall to the lot of man, on account of his faithfulness to God are by no means to be considered as *evils*; on the contrary, the admonition is to "rejoice and be exceeding glad, for great is your reward in heaven." The statement of Jesus is, that "in the world ye have tribulation, but in me ye have peace;" and although the children of God may be stoned or sawn asunder, although they may be destitute, afflicted and tormented, yet they have the assurance that "all things work together for good, to them that fear God."

It is certainly true, that "whatever the righteous man doeth shall prosper," but this is by no means a promise, that the prosperity shall be immediate,—he is casting bread upon the waters all through his life-pilgrimage; and although he has the assurance that it shall be gathered after many days, he has no promise of seeing all the fruits of his labors this side of the kingdom of God.

126. Wordly Prosperity a Reward of Righteousness and a Blessing.—There is no man that hath left house, or brethren, or sisters, or father, or mother, or wife, or children, or lands, for my sake and the gospel's, but he shall receive a hundred fold *now* in this time, houses, and brethren, and sisters, and mothers, and children, and lands.—Mark 10: 29, 30. I have been young, and now am old; yet have I not seen the righteous forsaken, nor his seed begging bread.—Ps. 37 25. Blessed is the man that feareth the Lord. *Wealth* and *riches* shall be his house.—Ps. 112; 1, 3. If thou return unto the Almighty, thou shalt be built up........,,.Then shalt thou lay up gold as dust.—Job. 22; 23, 24. In the house of the righteous is much treasure.—Job 19: 7.

Worldly Prosperity a CURSE and a BAR TO FUTURE REWARD.—Blessed be ye poor.—Luke 6; 20. Lay not up for yourselves treasures upon earth........,,,For where your treasure is there will your heart be also, Matt. 6: 19, 21. And it came to pass that the *beggar* died, and was carried by the angels into Abraham's bosom.—Luke 16. 22. It is easier for a camel to go through the eye of a needle, than for a *rich* man to enter into the kingdom of God.—Matt. 19: 24. *Wo* unto you that are *rich!* for ye have received your consolation.—Luke 6: 24.

In relation to Mark 10: 29, 30, it must be borne in mind that it was a declaration made to the apostles, and alluded to their itinerant mode of life. They sacrificed their private case, and comfort, and spent their time in traveling from house to house, to teach the Word of life to their fellow men, and those among whom they labored, being filled with the love of God, became their relatives in the household of faith, and more than this, they appreciated their labor, and divided their substance with them, so that their necessary wants were supplied as well as if it had been all their own. Hence they were commanded to " Provide neither gold, silver, nor brass in your purses, nor scrip for your journey, neither two coats, neither shoes, nor yet staves."—Matt. 10: 9, 10. It must be remembered however, that it was with them as with all true children of God, whatever they received in this age, they received " with persecutions." Ps. 37: 25 is an expression indicative of God's love and care for his children. Truly, wealth and riches are in the house of the man who feareth the Lord ; but this does not necessarily imply that he shall be possessed of the gold and silver of earth, if he has the " pearl of great price" he is possessed of untold wealth, without the riches of the world, for " In the house of the righteous is much treasure." Job 22: 23, 24 is a statement made by Eliphaz to Job, and was it not literally true ? Job was rich in earthly goods before his temptation, and we read that " The Lord blessed the latter end of Job more than the beginning."—Job 42: 12.

The only text in the latter part of the proposition which seems to require any explanation at our hands is Matt. 19: 24. And of this it is only necessary to state, that the expression " It is easier for a camel to go through the eye of a needle " was a common saying among the Jews to

denote anything extremely rare and difficult.—
(See Lightfoot & Bagster.) And it must be evident to every observer, that it is much harder for a rich man to gain the inheritance of the saints, than for the poor, from the fact that it seems almost impossible to possess the riches of earth, and not set the affections upon them. There are so many temptations in their path, that the rich are apt to either become *miserly*, or give themselves up to the gratifications of the lust of the eye, and the pride of life ; and it is this class to whom it is said, " Wo unto you that are rich." But this, by no means, applies to those (of whom earth can still boast a few) who, considering themselves the stewards of God, use their means to his honor and glory.

127. *The Christian Yoke is Easy.*—Come unto me, all ye that labor and are heavy laden and I will give you rest. Take my yoke upon you.........For my yoke is *easy* and my burden is light.—Matt. 11: 28-30.

***The Christian Yoke is NOT Easy.*—**In the world ye shall have *ribulation* —John 16: 33. Yea, and all that will live Godly in Christ Jesus shall suffer *persecution.*—2 Tim. 3: 12. Whom the Lord loveth he chasteneth, and scourgeth every son whom he receiveth.........For if ye be without chastisement then ye are bastards and not sons.— Heb. 13; 6, 8.

These texts are beautifully explained by a single passage, " In me ye might have peace,— in the world ye shall have tribulation." Truly, the yoke of Christ is easy, and his burden is light, but we have the promise of persecution and tribulation in the world.

128. *The Fruit of God's Spirit is Love and Gentleness.*— The fruit of the spirit is *love*, peace, joy, *gentleness*, and goodness. Gal. 5: 22.

***The Fruit of God's Spirit is VENGEANCE and FURY.*—** And the spirit of the Lord came upon him and he *slew a thousand men.*—Jud. 15; 14. And it came to pass on the morrow that the evil spirit from God came upon Saul......and there was a javelin in Saul's hand. And Saul cast the javelin; for he said,: I will smite David even to the wall with it.—1 Sam. 10: 11

This proposition may also be clearly explained by a few words. It is certainly true, that the legitimate fruits of God's "spirit is love, peace, joy, gentleness, and goodness," but it must also be borne in mind that Jehovah is possessed of the spirit of *justice*, and it is *justice* alone which his enemies have to fear. It is the *spirit of justice* alone which dictates His decrees of destruction or desolation, to those who openly defy his power and blaspheme his name

129. Longevity ENJOYED by the Wicked.—Wherefore do the wicked live, become *old*, yea, are mighty in power? Their seed is established in their sight with them, and their offspring before their eyes.—Job 21: 7, 8. They [men of the world] are full of children and leave the rest of their substance to their babes.—Ps. 17: 14, Though a sinner do evil a hundred times and his days be prolonged, yet surely I know that it shall be well with them that fear God.—Eccl. 8: 12. But the sinner being a hundred years old shall be accursed.—Is. 65: 20.

Longevity DENIED to the Wicked.—But it shall not be well with the wicked, neither shall he prolong his days.—Eccl. 8; 13. Bloody and deceitful men shall *not live out half their days*.—Ps. 55: 23. The *years* of the wicked shall be *shortened*.—Prov. 10: 27. They [the hypocrites] *die in youth*.—Job 36: 14. Be not over much wicked neither be foolish; why shouldst thou die before thy time?—Eccl. 7: 17.

Although the wicked may, in this age, live *even longer* than the righteous it may truly be said of them, that they shall not prolong their days, that they shall not live out half their days, that their years shall be shortened, that they die in youth, and die before their time, inasmuch as they cannot receive the eternal life which is promised to the righteous. And surely the longevity of man, in this age, is but a span when compared with the endless ages of eternity. See Prop. 122.

130. POVERTY a Blessing.—*Blessed* be ye *poor*......... *Woe* unto you that are *rich!*—Luke 6: 20, 24. Hath not God chosen the *poor* of this world, rich in faith, and heirs of the kingdom.— Jam. 2: 5.

RICHES a Blesing.—The rich man's *wealth* is his strong tower, but the destruction of the poor is their poverty.—Prov. 10: 15. If thou return unto the Almighty then thou shalt be built up......... Thou shalt then lay up *gold* as dust.—Job 22: 23, 24. And the Lord blessed the latter end of Job more than the beginning, for he had *14,000* sheep, and *6,000* camels and a thousand yoke of oxen, and a thousand she asses.—Job 42: 12.

NEITHER Poverty NOR Riches a Blessing.—Give me neither poverty nor riches; feed me with food convenient for me; lest I deny thee and say, Who is the Lord? or lest I be poor and steal and take the name of God in vain.—Prov. 30: 8, 9.

We think this subject has been clearly explained, at some length, under the 126th proposition; we will, however, briefly notice. Prov. 10: 15, which, by the way, the infidel has not quoted correctly, the Bible reads as follows, "The rich man's wealth is his strong city," which teaches that those who are rich, generally put their trust in their riches, instead of trusting in the Lord of the whole earth. This is illustrated by Psalms 52: 7, "Lo, this is the man that hath not made God his strength, but trusted in the abundance of his riches, and strengthed himself in his wickedness."

See also Prov. 18: 11, "The rich man's wealth is his strong city... *in his own conceit,*" surely nothing can make the subject plainer than this single text. We read also in Job 31: 24, 28, "If I have made gold my hope, or have said to the fine gold, Thou art my confidence.... This also were an iniquity to be punished by the judge."— We learn, therefore, that while wealth is an actual blessing to those who use their money to the honor, and glory of God—it is a terrible curse to those who hoard their means with miserly care, or consume it upon the vanities of earth.

131. *Wisdom a Source of ENJOYMENT.*—*Happy* is the man that findeth *wisdom*......... Wisdom's ways are ways of pleasantness and all her paths are peace.—Prov. 3: 13, 17.

Wisdom a Source of VEXATION, GRIEF and SORROW.—And I gave my heart to know wisdom......... I perceived that this also was vexation of spirit. For in much wisdom is much *grief.* and he that increaseth knowledge, increaseth sorrow.—Eccl. 7: 16.

It is evident that there are two different kinds of wisdom here referred to, and the matter is so clearly explained by the inspired James, that we cannot do better than to refer this proposition *entirely* to him. Please read. "Who is a wise man, and endued with knowledge among you? Let him show out of a good conversation, his works with meekness of wisdom. But if ye have bitter envying and strife in your hearts, glory not and lie not against the truth. This wisdom descendeth not from above, but is earthly, sensual, devilish. . . . But the wisdom that is from above is first pure, then peaceable, gentle, easy to be entreated, full of mercy and good fruits, without partiality, and without hypocrisy." James 3: 13, 17. Surely, no explanation of our's can make the matter plainer.

132. *A Good Name a BLESSING.*—A good name is better than precious ointment.—Eccl. 7: 1. A good name is rather to be chosen than great riches.—Prov. 22: 1.

A Good Name is a CURSE.—Wo unto you when all men shall speak well of you.—Luke 6: 26.

Surely, "a good name is better than precious ointment," and "rather to be chosen than great riches," but we must consider what kind of a name would be called *good* by the great "Father of light." To have the good name here spoken of, a man must maintain a character of strict honor and integrity; he must be known to the world as the unflinching advocate of the *right*, as the vindica-

tor of the oppressed, and the benefactor of the
needy ; then indeed he will have a *good name.*—
Still he will be *despised* by the worldly-wise, and
hated by the enemies of God, and his truth. " If
ye were of the world, the world would love its
own ; but because ye are not of the world, but
because I have chosen you out of the world, therefore the world hateth you." John 15: 19.

And well may there be a *woe* pronounced
against those, concerning whom *all men* will
speak well; for popularity among the masses can
only be obtained by those who sacrifice *principle*
for *fame,* who will sell *honor* for applause, and
wear the false face of flattery—those who forfeit
truth for renown, and pamper the faults and fol-
lies of mankind. And upon such unprincipled,
fawning sycophants of the world's favor, the woes
and judgments of God are pronounced.

133. *Laughter COMMENDED.*—To everything there is a season, a time to weep and a time to *laugh.*—Eccl. 3: 1, 4. Then I commended mirth, because a man hath no better thing under the sun
than to eat and to drink, and to be *merry.*—Eccl. 8: 15.

***Laughter CONDEMNED.*—**Wo unto you that laugh now.
Luke 6: 25. Sorrow is better than laughter ; for by the sadness of
countenance the heart is made better. The heart of the wise is in
the house of mourning; but the heart of the fool is in the house of
mirth.—Eccl. 7: 3, 4.

In the first two texts here quoted, innocent mirth
is commended. They are a recommendation of a
moderate use of worldly things, with a cheerful
and contented mind, but Luke 6: 25, alludes to the
foolish mirth of rioting and dissipation. See Prov.
5: 4. Prov. 14: 13. Eccl. 2: 2. " For as the
crackling of thorns under a pot so is the laughter
of a fool." Eccl. 7: 6. The ease of distinction between the two, is only equaled by the *absurdity* of
the objection.

134. *The Rod of CORRECTION a Remedy for Foolishness.*—Foolishness is bound in the heart of a child, but the rod of correction will drive it far from him.—Prov. 22: 15.

There is NO Remedy for Foolishness.—Though thou shouldst bray a fool in a mortar,..........yet will not his foolishness depart from him.—Prov. 27: 22.

It requires but little discrimination to see the harmony of the two texts above quoted. The first is certainly true, and that the last is equally so, *we know from experience.* The rod of correction will drive foolishness from the heart of a *child*, but you may bray a *fool* in a mortar, and yet his foolishness will not depart from him. Cannot the skeptic distinguish the difference between a *child* and a *fool?* Although the above proposition exhibts evident symptoms of *madness*, it certainly cannot be said of its author that " *much learning* hath made him *mad.*"

135. *A Fool Should be Answered According to his Folly.*—Answer a fool according to his folly.—Prov. 26: 4.

A Fool Should NOT be Answered According to his Folly.—Answer *not* a fool according to his folly.—Prov. 26: 5.

The following from Bishop Warburton on this point, is so satisfactory that we will quote it entire. " Had this advice been given simply, and without circumstances to answer the fool, and not to answer him, one would suppose that the different directions referred to the doing a thing *in and out of season,* but the matter is clearly explained. 1. The reason given why a fool should *not* be answered according to his folly, is, lest he (the answerer) should be like unto him. 2. The reason given why the fool should be answered according to his folly, is, lest he (the fool) should be wise in his own conceit. 1. The cause for *forbidding* to answer, therefore plainly insinuates that the defender of religion should not imitate the insulter of it, in his modes of disputation, which may be comprised in sophistry buffoonery and scurrility. 2. The cause assigned for directing to answer, &c., as plainly intimates that the sage should address himself, to confute the fool upon his own false principles, by showing that they lead to conclusions very wide from, and very opposite to, those impieties he would deduce from them. If *anything* can allay a fool's vanity, and prevent his being wise in his own conceit, it must be the dishonor of having his own principles turned against himself, and shown to be destructive to his own conclusions." Treatise on Grace—Preface.

136. *Temptation to be Desired.*—My brethren, count it all joy when ye fall into temptation.—Jas. 1: 2.

***Temptation NOT to be Desired.*—**Lead us *not* into temptation — Matt. 6: 13.

Matt. 6: 13, literally translated from the Greek, reads as follows: "Abandon us not to temptation, but preserve us from evil," and the evident idea, of the petition is, that God will not forsake his children while struggling with temptation, but strengthen and aid them by his grace, that they may be able to *endure*, instead of yielding to it. See 1 Cor. 10: 13. "There hath no temptation taken you but such as is common to man; but God is faithful, who will not suffer you to be tempted above that ye are able ; but will with the *temptation* also make a way to escape, that ye may be able to bear it." Hence, James 1: 2, is exactly in point. "My brethren count it all joy when ye fall into divers temptations, knowing this, that the *trying* of your faith worketh patience;" for "Blessed is the man that endureth temptation ; for when he is tried, he shall receive the crown of life, which the Lord hath promised

to them that love him." See ver. 12. We can
conceive of nothing more beautifully harmonious,
than these texts are, when allowed their proper
weight and meaning.

137. *Prophecy is Sure.*—We have also a more *sure word of
prophecy*, whereunto we do well that we take heed, as unto a light
that shineth in a dark place.—2 Pet. 1: 19.

Prophecy is NOT Sure.—At what instant I shall speak concerning a nation, and concerning a kingdom, to pluck up, and to pull
down, and to destroy it; if that nation against whom I have pronounced turn from their evil, I will *repent* of the evil that I thought
to do unto them. And at what instant I shall speak concerning a
a nation and concerning a kingdom. to build and to plant it; if it
do evil in my sight, that it obey not my voice, then I will *repent* of
the good wherewith I said I would benefit them.—Jer. 18: 7-10.

Nothing can be surer than the prophecies of
Jehovah—events which He has foretold through
his prophets are just as certain, as those which
have already taken place, and in this consists one
of the strongest bulwarks of the christian religion.
Infidels have madly attacked the prophecies of
the Bible, but the massive walls of truth, are so
impregnable that their blows have scarcely pro-
duced an echo.

The idea that Jer. 18: 7, 10, conflicts with the
foregoing position, on the certainty of the fulfillment of prophecy, cannot for a moment be sustained; While Peter is speaking of prophecy,
alone, Jeremiah refers to nothing but *promises*
and *threatenings*, which are not prophecies; Divine government is based upon the principles of
eternal justice. He may have threatened to
pluck up, and destroy a nation for its sins, but
his promise is, that if that nation turn from their
evil, the hand of Infinite Mercy, will arrest the
threatened judgment; but if on the contrary, he
has prepared to build up a nation, and it does evil
in his sight, and proves unworthy of this care, the

voice of justice decrees that they shall *not receive* the benefits which they have *forfeited*. Hence the judgments and promises to the nations of the earth are *conditional*, but the sure word of prophecy is *unalterable*.

138. *Man's Life was to be ONE HUNDRED and TWEN-TY Years.*—His days shall be one hundred and twenty years.—Gen. 6: 3.

Man's Life is but SEVENTY Years.—The days of our years are three score years and ten.—Ps. 90: 10.

It is claimed that there is a discrepancy existing between Gen. 6: 3 and Ps. 90: 10. The former promising a life of one hundred and twenty years and the other a life of only seventy. A satisfactory solution of this apparent difficulty is found in the fact that Gen. 6: 3 has specific reference to the generation immediately preceding the flood, whose probation was to continue for just that length of time. It was just one hundred and twenty years from the time that God revealed his purpose unto Noah, until the destruction of that generation. Hence this text is purely of a *local* character, and refers to that period alone.

139. *The Fear of Man was to be upon EVERY BEAST.* The fear of you and the dread of you shall be on every beast of the earth.—Gen. 9; 2.

The Fear of Man is NOT upon the LION.—A lion turneth not away for any.—Prov. 30: 30.

There are but few things better calculated to try the patience of the honest investigator than objections to God's Word like the one given above, for every principle of honor and candor is here grossly violated. In quoting Prov. 30: 30 the skeptic has *wilfully* omitted the explanatory passage—we say wilfully because the design is

so evident that we cannot impute it to ignorance.
Please read the whole verse. " A lion which is
strongest among beasts and turneth not away for
any." Hence we learn the true idea of the text,
i. e., that the lion turneth not away for *any beast.*
But we find in the above proposition that the explanatory clause is left out without even the sign
of omission, and we ask our readers in all candor,
what must be the character of the cause which
requires such perversions of God's Word in order
to sustain it? What claim can a man have to our
confidence or respect, who thus blasphemes the
God of the Universe by wilfully perverting His
words?

140. Miracles a Proof of Divine Mission.—Now when John
had heard in the prison the works of Christ, he sent two of his disciples, and said unto him, Art thou he that should come, or do
we look for another? Jesus answered and said unto them, Go and
show John again those things which yo do hear and see; the blind
receive their sight, and the lame walk, the lepers are cleansed, and
the deaf hear, the dead are raised.—Matt. 11: 2-5. Rabbi, we know
that thou art a teacher come from God; for no man can do these
miracles that thou doest except God be with him.—John 3: 2. And
Israel saw that great work which the Lord done upon the Egyptians:
and the people feared the Lord and believed the Lord and his servant Moses.—Ex. 14: 31.

141. Miracles NOT a Proof of Divine Mission.—And Aaron
cast down his rod before Pharaoh, and before his servants and it became a serpent. Then Pharaoh also called the wise men and the
sorcerers: now the magicians of Egypt, *they also did in like manner*
with their enchantments, for they cast down every man his rod, and
they became serpents.—Ex. 7: 10-12. If there arise among you a
prophet, or a dreamer of dreams, and giveth thee a sign or a wonder,
and the sign or the wonder come to pass wherein he spake unto
thee, saying, Let us go after other gods which thou hast not known,
and let us serve them, thou shalt not hearken unto the words of that
prophet or that dreamer of dreams.—Deut. 13: 1-3. If I by Beelze-
bub *cast out devils*, by whom do *your sons* cast them out?-Luke 6: 19.

In relation to Ex. 7: 10, 12 it seems only necessary to remark that as Egypt was remarkably

addicted to magic) sorcery, &c., it was necessary
that God should permit Pharaoh's wise men to
act to the utmost of their skill. They were allowed to imitate the work of God, that his superiority
might be clearly seen, and the credibility of his
servants established beyond a doubt, and this was
fully done when "Aaron's rod swallowed up their
rods." Why did not the infidel quote *this* portion
of the Divine testimony also! Evidently because
this would have paralyzed the idea which he was
endeavoring to convey.

Deut. 13: 1, 3 is a warning against false prophets and dreamers, or those who pretend that
they have received supernatural instruction in
their night visions; hence the text has no bearing
whatever upon miracles.

The next text is a misquotation; it is found in
Matt. 12: 27 instead of Luke 6: 19. Dr. Clarke
remark's upon this subject as follows:

Children or sons of the prophets, mean the
disciples of the prophets; and the children or
sons of the Pharisees, disciples of the Pharisees.
From Acts 19: 13, 14, it is evident there were
exorcists among the Jews, and from our Lord's
saying here it is also evident, that the disciples of
the Pharisees did cast out demons, or at least
*those who educated them, wishes to have it believed
that they had such a power.* Our Lord's argument here is extremely conclusive; if the man
who cast out demons, proves himself thereby to
be in league with, and influenced by Satan, then
your disciples, and you who taught them, are all
of you in league with the Devil; you must either
give up your assertion, that I cast demons by Be-
elzebub, or else admit this conclusion, in its fullest
force and latitude, that ye are *all* children of the
devil, and leagued with him against God.

In order to be a proof of a divine mission, a miracle must have the approval of the Deity, and no

miracle will be approved of Him, which does not recognize Him as its Author.

142. *Moses Was a Very MEEK Man.*—Now, the man Moses, was very meek, above all the men upon the face of the earth, Num. 12: 3.

***Moses Was a Very CRUEL Man.*—**And Moses said unto them, Have ye saved all the women alive?......Now, therefore, kill every male among the little ones, and kill every woman that hath known a man.—Num. 31: 15, 17.

Truly "Moses was very *meek*, above all the men that were upon the face of the earth. He was a humble and faithful servant of the Most High, and as such he executed the commands of Jehovah. In relation to the Midianites, it is only necessary to state that God himself commanded their extirmination. *Moses was not the cause of it.* He only executed the commands of God, and was accountable to Him alone. Hence, the part that he bore in the matter has no bearing upon his character, and although he may have been unwilling to inflict pain or death upon the criminals, he could but vindicate the *justice* of Jehovah in the act. Surely, a good reason is given for slaying the women of Midian. Please read the connection, "And Moses said unto them, Have ye saved all the women alive? Behold *these* caused the children of Israel, through the counsel of Balaam, to commit trespass against the Lord, in the matter of Peor, and there was a plague among the congregation of the Lord." See Num. 25: 2. Num. 24: 14. 2 Pet. 2: 15. Rev. 2: 14. Num. 25: 9.

In relation to the killing of the male children, we will merely remark that it was a thousand times better for *them*, and for the world that they should be cut off in infancy than to grow up in rejection of God, and in the wilful idolatry of the

Midianites.   The skeptic is very sensitive upon
the subject of God's judgments against the trans-
gressors of His laws.

143. ELIJAH Went up to Heaven.—And Elijah went up by a
whirlwind into *heaven.*—2 Kings 2: 11.

NONE BUT CHRIST ever Ascended into Heaven.—*No man
hath ascended up to heaven* but he that came down from heaven,
even the Son of Man.—John 3: 13.

In John 3: 13, it is evident that the expression,
ascend up to Heaven, signifies *to search into and
to understand the counsel of God.* See Newcome, Raphelius, and Dr. Doddridge.   The same
idea is conveyed in Deut. 30: 12, in the expression
"Who shall go up for us into Heaven, and bring
it (the word) unto us, that we may hear it and do
it ?" also, in Rom. 10: 6, " Say not in thine heart
who shall ascend into Heaven?" and in Prov.
30: 4, "Who hath ascended up into Heaven."—
The statement has no reference to a physical ascension, but obviously refers to that moral excel-
lence and divine knowledge, possessed alone by
the Son of God.   Hence, the literal ascension of
Elijah, by no means militates against the statement of John concerning the Messiah.

144. All Scripture is Inspired.—*All Scripture* is given by *inspiration* of God.—2 Tim. 3: 16.

Some Scripture is NOT Inspired.—But I speak this by permis
sion and not by commandment.—1 Cor. 7: 6. But to the rest speak
I. not the Lord.—1 Cor. 7: 12. That which I speak, I speak it not
after the Lord.—2 Cor. 11: 17.

In the sentence, " All Scripture is given by
inspiration of God," it might be well for the infidel to notice that the word " IS," was inserted by
the translators, so that the text by no means spec-
ifies *what* Scripture is inspired.   The word
scripture is derived from *scribo* to write, and
merely means *a writing* or *anything written.* The

idea of the text under consideration is, that " All writing given by inspiration of God is profitable for doctrine," &c., and certainly never intended to convey the idea that *all writing* is inspired by God, but simply that, *all writing which is given by inspiration of God, is profitable.*

We have now patiently followed the skeptic through his entire series of one hundred and forty-four propositions, wherein he claims that God's word contradicts itself; and we find that his *last* objection to the Bible is as groundless as the *first*, while we have, we trust, fairly and satisfactorily removed them all. Infidels are often ingenious, and they have in many instances, woven an artful web whereby to cover the truth, which at first sight is well calculated to deceive; but they *never have* and *never can* present an objection to God's word, which the light of fair and honest investigation will not quickly dispel.

In the foregoing propositions we have found many texts, in which the apparent obscurity of the language, has furnished an opportunity for cavil; and we cannot wonder that a want of harmony is supposed to exist between them, by one who has never studied God's word, or investigated the plan of Jehovah. Other propositions we have found, which could only have originated in the *grossest ignorance*, and others still, we regret to say, which can but be attributed to vile *dishonesty*; for in these instances, the Bible has been so *meanly perverted*, and every principle of honor and manliness so *shamefully violated*, that with all our charity, we CANNOT cover the offence with the mantle of ignorance.

Hence, in looking back over the work we have reviewed, we conclude that the skeptic only needs more *information*, and more *honesty*, to make him a rational believer of God's Word.

APPENDIX.

———◦•◦———

It was our original intention to write in con nection with the present work a somewhat lengthy article on the authenticity of the Holy Scriptures. But our libraries are enriched by so many *valuaable* works upon the subject, that any attempt of our's would not only appear weak, but surperfluous. So far as labored arguments and eloquent appeals are concerned, the christian literature of the present day is indeed rich. To those, however, who are *willing* to *investigate* the claims of the Bible, allow us to suggest the most tempting field of research that was ever presented to the mind of a student. We refer to the study of prophecy in connection with the record of the Historian. This is a theme which can never become uninteresting, for the prophecies of the Old Testament point to the infallibility of God's Word with mathematical precision; they present the *evidences* of revelation so clearly, that infidelity stands appalled before the rich developments of truth. The mighty walls of ancient kingdoms, and the magnificent temples of antiquity, are the monuments of God's eternal truth. One hundred and sixty years before an enemy's foot had ever entered Babylon, the *complete* desolation of the *Lady of Kingdoms*, was foretold by the inspired penman. At the time when she was the " glory of the Chaldees' excellency"—when her mighty walls and brazen gates bade defiance to the united armies of the earth—even then the eye of the prophet looked down through the long aisles of the ages, and in the clear light of inspiration, he read even the *name* of the man before whose mandates her glory should fade. So accurate are these predictions that the testimony of those who witnessed the desolate scene in after centuries, appears like a repetition of the words of the prophet.

Read the eloquent descriptions of the overthrow of Babylon, as found in the rich language of Isaiah, or the mournful wail of Jeremiah; then turn to the classic pages of Xenophon and Herodotus, and they will be found to be but the *echos* of inspiration.

In reference to the destruction of Jerusalem, the testimony of Josephus is a mere *commentary* upon the predictions recorded in Lev. and Deut. Read the prophecies concerning Samaria, Ammon, Moab, Idumea, Tyre, and Egypt. They are clothed in the glowing eloquence of Isaiah, Jeremiah, Ezekiel, Hosea, Amos, and Micah.— The burning words of ancient truth still gleam upon the sacred page, and the testimony of hundreds of modern travelers, confirm their perfect accuracy. The pages of the standard works in all our libraries, record the *literal* fulfillment of those prophecies which were traced upon the sacred scroll, in the distant ages of antiquity. Strabo and Rollin are witnesses for God. Even Gibbon, the highly gifted but *infidel* Historian, unconsciously testifies in every volume, to the truth of Divine Revelation. And Voltaire, in the account of his extensive travels, is also an unwilling witness to the veracity of the sacred writers.— But we can only *suggest* this fascinating theme to the student, with the *earnest* desire that he will give it that attention which it so richly deserves.

We wish, however, before bidding farewell to our readers, to give, from the best authority we have, some of the causes of *apparent* discrepancies in the Holy Oracles. We beg leave to introduce the following thoughts from Dr. Sleigh, which we consider valuable to the Bible student:

CAUSES OF APPARENT DISCREPANCIES.—Had the writers of the New Testament undertaken, or proposed to undertake, to give a full account of all the circumstances connected with the birth, life, death, and resurrection of their Divine Master; and had any one of them failed in so doing, such failure, even in one point, would be fatal to the veracity of the narrator, and consequently fatal, so far as *he* was concerned, to the truth of Christianity. But so far from any one of them professing to give a detail of all that related to Christ, not one of them professed that he was even writing a common history of Him. And so far from their having had any such idea, the Apostles in the conclusion of that Gospel, which may be considered as having been *attested to by them all*, (when they said of its Author, "This is the disciple which testifieth of these things, and wrote these things, *and* WE *know that his testimony is true*;" John 21: 24,) they figuratively express their conviction of *the little*, in proportion to what might have been, recorded; (ver. 25.) And Luke, who has written more than all of them, says, that his gospel related to what Jesus had only *began* to do and teach. Acts 1: 1. The fact is, the gospels, (as they are called) are only *memoirs*, composed of detached narrations of circumstances, put down by the sacred writers, and witnesses, just as they appeared to their judgment, of most importance. Had these men written in the contrary way; had they agreed verbatim in their histories of Christ, infidels would immediately cry out, "see they wrote in concert; there was evidently a collusion between them—it is all a job,"

&c. That such would have been the language of
infidels is manifest; for where there is the least
similarity between the sacred writers, as for instance in the account given by Matthew and
Mark of the fig tree, and the destruction of Jerusalem, they immediately shout, " Collusion! Collusion!" We maintain, that so far from the Gospels having in them any thing which invalidates
the veracity of their authors, or proves either craft,
dishonesty, design, or enthusiasm, that they in-
controvertibly prove the very reverse of each of
these qualities, exhibiting the very best possible
test of the truth of human testimony, viz: *Sub-
stantial truth under circumstantial variety.*" All
the apparent discrepancies in the Bible, (*for rec-
ollect we deny that there is a single actual contradiction,*) may be (according to Horne) referred to
one or other of the following causes:

1. To the different sourses whence the inspired
writers drew their narratives. Thus, while the
twelve apostles were absent from Christ, some of
them longer, some shorter, as they went two by two,
some must have witnessed what others did not, and
vice versa.

2. To the different designs which the sacred writers
had in the composition of their narratives : *e. g.* the
ganealogy of Christ given by Matthew and Luke.—
The former being for the Jews, the latter for the
Gentiles.

3. To the liability of the names of persons and
places changing.

4. The name of the head of a tribe or nation was
sometimes given to their posterity : *e. g.*, Edom or
Esau is put for the Edomites, who were the descendants of Esau. Num. 20; 18.

5. The same persons or places sometimes had several names : *e. g.*, Esau's wife is called Bashemath in
Gen. 26: 34 and Adah in Gen. 36: 2. Thus he who
was nominated for the apostleship is called Justus,

Joseph and Barnabas (Acts 1: 25); Joses and Barnabas are the names of the same apostle. The place called Emishphat and Kadesh, Gen. 14: 7. Magdala, in Matt. 15: 39, is called Dalmanutha in Mark 8: 10; and the country of the Gergesenes, in Matt. 8: 28, is called in Mark 5: 1, Gadarenes.

6. To many persons and places having the same name. There was one Bethlehem in the tribe of Zebulun (Josh. 19: 15), and another in the tribe of Judah. Matt. 2: 6. Luke 2: 4. There were two towns called Cana (Josh. 19: 28. John 2: 1); several Cæsareas, several Zechariahs and several Herods.

7. Things oftentimes related in different order.

8. Events introduced by anticipation. Creation of man (Gen. 1: 27), which, after several other things inserted, is related more at large in the creation of Adam. Gen. 2: 7, 21, 23.

9. The sacred writers sometimes speak in general, or round numbers We do the same at the present day, without the least intention of deception.

10. Sometimes numbers are exclusive, sometimes inclusive.

11. The writers sometimes quote numbers from the Septuagint, and sometimes from the Hebrew texts.

12. Some events are referred to (not as to where,) by the sacred writers of the New Testament, which are not noticed by the inspired historians of the Old, but which nevertheless, might be in other records then extant..

13. Kings and their sons frequently reigned at the same time during the Hebrew monarchy; hence chronological discrepancies.

14. Sometimes historians adopted different methods of computation, assigning different dates to the same period; e. g., in Gen. 15: 13 it is announced to Abraham that his "seed should be a stranger in a land that was not theirs, and should serve them, and that they should afflict them FOUR HUNDRED YEARS;" but in

Ex. 12: 40. 41 it is said, "They dwelt in Egypt four hundred and THIRTY years." Both are perfectly consistent; the apparent contradiction arising from the computation being made from TWO different dates.— In Genesis the time is calculated from the date of the promise to Abraham of a son; and in Exodus from his departure from Ur of the Chaldees.

Finally, while we cheerfully admit that there are numerous *apparent* contradictions in the sacred Scriptures, we positively deny that there is a single positive contradiction in the whole Bible. Moreover, we assert, that the greater the number of apparent contradictions, the greater is the proof that it never was made up by one man; that it never was the result of collusion; and finally, that it never was invented by any man or men, with a view to deceive mankind.

INDEX TO SUBJECTS.

———————•♦•———————

It will be seen that the following index refers to those points, which the infidel claims are both affirmed and denied in the Sacred Oracles.

THEOLOGICAL DOCTRINES.

MORAL PRECEPTS.

HISTORICAL FACTS.

SPECULATIVE DOCTRINES.

CPSIA information can be obtained
at www.ICGtesting.com
Printed in the USA
BVHW03s2308180418
513722BV00021B/644/P